THE SUITCASE TREE

Filip Marinovich

the operating system print//document

THE SUITCASE TREE

ISBN: 978-1-946031-34-1
Library of Congress Control Number: 2018915125
copyright © 2019 by Filip Marinovich
edited and designed by ELÆ [Lynne DeSilva-Johnson] with the author.

is released under   a Creative Commons CC-BY-NC-ND (Attribution, Non Commercial, No Derivatives) License: its reproduction is encouraged for those who otherwise could not afford its purchase in the case of academic, personal, and other creative usage from which no profit will accrue.

Complete rules and restrictions are available at:
http://creativecommons.org/licenses/by-nc-nd/3.0/

For additional questions regarding reproduction, quotation, or to request a pdf for review contact operator@theoperatingsystem.org

This text was set in Helvetica Neue, Mank Sans, DK Dirrrty, Franchise, and OCR-A Standard.

The cover uses an original piece by Filip Marinovich.

Books from The Operating System are available directly from the publisher and distributed to the trade directly via Ingram, with production by Spencer Printing, in Honesdale, PA, in the USA.

the operating system

www.theoperatingsystem.org
operator@theoperatingsystem.org

THE SUITCASE TREE

2018-19 OS System Operators

CREATIVE DIRECTOR/FOUNDER: ELÆ [Lynne DeSilva-Johnson]
DEPUTY EDITOR: Peter Milne Greiner
CONTRIBUTING EDITOR, EXSPECPO: Kenning JP Garcia
CONTRIBUTING EDITOR, FIELD NOTES: Adrian Silbernagel
CONTRIBUTING EDITOR, IN CORPORE SANO: Amanda Glassman
CONTRIBUTING EDITOR, GLOSSARIUM: Ashkan Eslami Fard
CONTRIBUTING EDITOR, GLOSSARIUM / RESOURCE COORDINATOR:
Bahaar Ahsan
JOURNEYHUMAN / SYSTEMS APPRENTICE: Anna Winham
DIGITAL CHAPBOOKS / POETRY MONTH COORDINATOR: Robert Balun
TYPOGRAPHY WRANGLER / DEVELOPMENT COORDINATOR: Zoe Guttenplan
DESIGN ASSISTANTS: Lori Anderson Moseman, Orchid Tierney, Michael Flatt
SOCIAL SYSTEMS / HEALING TECH: Curtis Emery
VOLUNTEERS and/or ADVISORS: Adra Raine, Alexis Quinlan, Clarinda Mac Low, Bill Considine, Careen Shannon, Joanna C. Valente, L. Ann Wheeler, Erick Sáenz, Knar Gavin, Joe Cosmo Cogen, Sarah Doughterty

The Operating System is a member of the Radical Open Access Collective, a community of scholar-led, not-for-profit presses, journals and other open access projects. Now consisting of 40 members, we promote a progressive vision for open publishing in the humanities and social sciences.

Learn more at: http://radicaloa.disruptivemedia.org.uk/about/

Your donation makes our publications, platform and programs possible!
We <3 You.
http://www.theoperatingsystem.org/subscribe-join/

ALSO BY FILIP MARINOVICH

Zero Readership (2008)
And If You Don't Go Crazy I'll Meet You Here Tomorrow (2011)
Wolfman Librarian (2015)

To Cecilia Wu
To my parents

And in memory of Uncle Dragon

CONTENTS

    The Suitcase Tree   11

UNCLE DRAGON REQUIEM
    Dragan and Branka   15
    When Uncle Dragon Passed   16

UNCLE DRAGON REMAINS
    Dogens and Dragons   23
    Manic Mixture 8 from Outer Space   26
    Jeudi Da Sensorium Rum   30
    Vendredi Samadhi Starring Sandra Dee   34
    On Fucking Reality   34

THE FUNERAL MIME SPEAKS FROM THE ASTEROID CHIRON
    Obi Wan Threnody   43
    Posthumous Puberty Protein Powder   45
    Virgo to the Two Pisceans   47
    The Sinking of the Tectonic   51
    The Necrophile Tourguide   53
    Uncle Lungs   57
    Job Interview with Maker   59
    Anasamadhi Pathology   62

TWENTY FOUR HOURS WITH FRANCIS BACON IN THE CHESTNUT TREE OF HEAVEN
    Cinnamon Theremin   73
    Lava   74
    Francis Bacon Critiques my Painting   75
    Between the Globes   78
    Thrownness Duet   93

"FOR OCCUPATION—THIS"

Dear Autodefenestrated Self	99
George Washington Pisces	102
From the Daybooks of Fasterbean Damages	104
Fasterbean Damages	107
Between the Heaves of Storm	110
Shakespearian Motley College	112

PARTNERS WITH THE TREES

A Sectary Astronomical	119
At Veselka	122
Coyote Bananas	125
Lavender Bender for Joanne Kyger	130
Dogen's Two Thrownnesses	137
Hamlet Le Pendu	140
Manic Mixture 7 Failures in the Fish	124
Hockney Water	146
Mercredi Skiis	148
The Halibut Arms	150
Sleeping Through the Days and Communicating with Emigre Friends	153
Synopsis Cyclops	157
Why I Am Not Straight	159
Red Condom in the Ramble	161
Pigeontimacy	163
Dear Mom	170

FOUR DAYS IN BELGRADE JFK

Airport Diner with Mother	177
My Aunt Architecture	178
Over International Cellphone	180
Email from Belgrade	181

TRIPTYCH IN CAPRICORN, AQUARIUS, AND PISCES

Absent Sophia	193
Count Mouth	198
School of Silencers	201

BACKMATTER 203

THE SUITCASE TREE

Tree
    in
Saint Mark's
      churchyard
  one
 rollaway
  suitcase
hangs from
  your most
    crooked
   branch bicep
I name you
  The Suitcase Tree
though really your name is Walter Benjamin
          you say
  and your business
    is to grow
       luminous rectangular
         suitcase fruit
     from graves.

UNCLE DRAGON REQUIEM

DRAGAN AND BRANKA

We were just talking about his shoes:
"New shoes," he said
"Just in time for Branka to bury me in them."

WHEN UNCLE DRAGON PASSED

Now what? He asked. We could jump
From rock to rock.
Uncle Dragon lime green triangle flags
Or blankets
Dry on the terrace
Beside the—
Ortogonal to the
Rusted blue scaffolding bars
And plywood planks. How large.
Three buttons. You are super fast
To undo them
But what then.
So therefore
Very nice to meet you.
I haven't seen you in twelve years
And now you're dead
And then you guys did the mile.
Light a candle tomorrow.
Cremation Wednesday.
I light an orange candle
With several striped shades of bluegreen wax
Grooving through it
Crowning like an infant
The new colors are born
Unnameable
And will have to fend for themselves
Before orientation weekend with parents
With larynx.
Ooh. Don't try to impress me just think.
The last fireflies of the the season lie to me
They are the first again. Nothing previously
Thought can be repeated. *Potchemou?*
Patchymuse.
Motley cruiserfish.

I'm going to kiss
The dusky paths of Entrail Park Palace.
This is the last stop in the park
Please leave the park now.
The crunch underfoot is fastforwarded to Thursday.
What is the cream of the river now crematorium rigormortis
Oratorio menace sheetmusic tube telescope
As poetry must never be used for the microscope
Ways it was intended for
For anything used for its own purpose
Lacks perversity, the only cure for
Utility capitalism.

Electric protein perversity
Better than biodiversity
Windmills at the edge of a grey flooded field of famine.
There's a bear tongue cut off of
Your trophy apron.
The beginning of that Saturday
Is moleskin trouser leg loose and open
For anything but legs.
Put the botch on it.
Last minute is my senior year.
What if we did it at Union Station New Haven?
Create jobs. Burn in an insurance fire
like heirloom furniture at dawn.
Can you put your leg on the same step you're sitting on?

No I just don't know what to do with this arm.
Next week I can go running so fast I grow an orange crow beak.
Heckle and Jeckle will be my foreskin attendants
As I undress my pink turtleneck pecker for the first time
since castration.

Auto-castration, that is,
The only carpool worth following up on over the George Washington Bridge that
Must cut down the cherry tree just like its namesake
The Father of our Immobilities and their bomb test island territories.

I resign my post as nephew
So my water tower uncle can find me
A person who can sing him
Across in a bardo boat. A bong load.

UNCLE DRAGON REMAINS

DOGENS AND DRAGONS

Zeitmindfullgeist

DOGENS AND DRAGONS

Timemindfullguest. The wind of the guest blows in and we are busy building walls against the undocumented guestworker Irma.

How did that work out for ya, Plutocrat?

But these are obvious slob maneuvers, my specialty.

"The body as a skinbag," now that's a little tougher. Or when my brother Al drinks a sixpack of Miller Highlife in Los Angeles, and I, sober two years now, get drunk in New York. Such is the tolerance of Interpenetrativeness, apartment complex.

But speaking of this particular skinbag temporary costume: ever since my mom came back from her last trip to Belgrade, the final visit with her now dead brother, Dragan, whom I call Uncle Dragon since childhood when he drove me through the Belgrade Yugoslavia streets speeding in his red Renault Diana, car of the Huntress and the Moongoddess of Virginity, which means Independence in the Mediterranean, not hymenese as in Puritanamerica...

My brother is from Amida, California, the West, where chestnut beer flows from the mountains that are walking and the skyscrapers flowing into the rivers. Even though this is so I do not believe I can control it: the heatwave logic is upon us again, and the mountains walk over us to show us they need footpaths too, and we are not the only ones who can clear a nature trail to return home for a hiking trip into the groove of bark and moss and redwood tinyhairs that love to be smoked by camping bears. Oh how I love those bears. I thought I could become one once before I lost all my weight and hair, but such is the sundance of a skinbag among the pears that drink in autumn, and the chrysanthemums drunk in spring.

Nevertheless, the mountains are walking, and the wood of Birnam walks on the White House and will not be appeased.

These are slobvious prophecies.

Nevertheless when my mom Lillian or Lillyanna got back from Beograd or Belgrade she brought her rollaway suitcase which I promptly appropriated from her. I wanted the aura of Belgrade around it. Now I drag it everywhere even though my Uncle Dragon is dead we are two skinbags. One walks the other. The rollaway suitcase is walking me and I never have to walk it, it is more convenient than a pup this way, but I walk it all the same when it is tired of walking me away from the mountains stepping on me. High stepping! The rollaway suitcase walks me and I walk it and the mountains are walking, do not doubt that they are walking, even though they do walk, it is not mere plate tectonics of which I talk, amateur geologist sleuther ghost. This sliding is different colliding. The Chrysler is walking to the East River and it bends down for a sip of water and recieves a nip on its nose from a fish! Fish! You know that thing when it's so hot you want to pass out but you refuse to go back inside your filing cabinet and die alone?

That's the way it is with me betimes. Because everything you see around you is time: the mountains walking, the East Side bluegreen glass skytoucher pedophiliac condominium complexes, and the West Side redbrick townhouse mountains walk out into the Green Mountains of Vermont and wash themselves in the cream of the long river flowing from the crematorium chimneyplume where Dogen Dragon watches his parents go up and I watch my Uncle Dragon and myself go up too. Skinbags are kites. But really they are smoke kites, or, we are, rather, we are cinder poof poof kites before long, so I like that we can bang our skinbags against each other like this, and get all the dust out of us before we are dust.

.   .   .   .

MANIC MIXTURE 8 FROM OUTER SPACE

No, that's a great department. Were there any pretty boys? Yes! But I can't touch them. I've come to this point where I've sublimated my myriad desires so much I can barely recognize them as they occur except I experience them as eruptions then. My name is Frank Throne. I first came into the world. Ego. In the red on red room of Wallace Stevens I was one of the thrones: was I the obvious red one or the little rocking chair frog babythrone. How does it feel to go from being a throne to passing as a fortytwoyearold nocturnal Odyssey initiate through the urn districts of dossier wallpaper New York. Do you remember the red food dye bathtub and Sara sticking your hand in it with her blue eyeshadow dripping down to her cheeks. I don't remember anything of anything of of. Ant hill district. Brickbrick. All the images of the world? Hardly: this is not a trapping mall. Memhorror, are we engaged? Are we going all the way? People try to intervene, to throw an enselfconsciousating light on what you do, to define it, when I don't know, and I need to not know, what it is I'm doing, which now is shot by a hunter in orange dayglo vest with pinned scalps of trumpwigheads dangling from the flapping lapels. Hunter knows best. And where is Artemis? The Lateral Travel Arts building closed down, it's cool, it's a space I like to fill, stop talking about it so I can keep listening without your interference. It's gone, do you hear yourself? Somewhere the monitor blew out, between Cambridge and Penn Station, and now this poem is called Fuck You to the Enshriners. I'm not dead yet. Though by your smiling you wish it so. Kill yourselves, governments, if you're so curious about death. "You look...thinner," old friends like to greet me these days. Do I need to make a T-shirt that says I'M NOT DYING I CHANGED MY DIET. Yes I clearly do. But my name is Frank Throne, not little froggy kiddy my rocking chair throne or encoded codeine in the Tylenol viking pills. But it's like the grandparent's day, I don't agree with any of this, O friends of the Atreiades Treehouse, O friends to this ground and liegemen to the Dane. Denmark leaves a wetmark on my bed when I wetdream of it through my penis. Maybe there is a road of mobmobmob cobbles that throws you off it and you land in the ditch of a new recording contract with Fasterbean Damages to produce you. What can go wrong, product-oriented guru. You're screaming. But I really love my friends, I feel closer to the baristas than I do to my friends, my friends keep me at a distance of three thousand mikes west and east so I don't blow out the mike amps of the Pacific and Adriatic coasts respectively. But Belgrade is landlocked now. The Panonian sea used to be washing up on Belgrade shores, then it dried up and pulled back to the Adriatic and Meditteranean Seas, it shrunk up in marshes and landfills and New Belgrade Fountains, victim of a shrink who could psychoanalyze whole seas away, Dr. Ecocide, responsibility of humans. (Me!) You're just irritable because you had a tiny taste of threeday travel last week and now you are back in your Denmark New York rut route cage and cannot venture forth again and be great. Tell us what you mean. What do you hear. What do you CVS mean what you hear CHASE DUANE READE DUENDE GREEN SPRITE AND DEATH THROAT MIKE hi Frank Throne hi Frank Throne hi Frank Throne hi. I've stationed here for some work, I'm Mercury, childgrater, need some children to grate over my spaghetti to give it that childblood taste, so good to see you. But I love my friends so much I don't have any, my students pay me to be my friends, the baristas are closer to my brains than a Denmark sentry to his tower. I don't mean to imply. Yes you do. Immolate yourself and see if you have "No Self" to immolate. Then who is that on top of the spear you see from a distance yes it's you bleeding red mussel stew into the bowl of the French gourmet come to collect your taxes from you so you won't feel so horny in the spring, it's a US gourmet tooth operator pulling the long incisor levers in the Dyre Wolfmouth hanging above the offal office where you conduct your international ash business with desk, intestines curtain, and phonemouth. Fury, Frank Throne, I was so inspired by this person because when I was his age I was doing dishes, I was I and io io ai ai io io ai ai Medea yoyo knocking Jason's skull to pieces with her marvelous stone yoyo, that's quite a thing, one exception, no violence, and yet I love my friends the bioluminescent sea algae seaweed who give me a runway in the Pangean sea to land on. Hi, I'm John Glenn, and this is the moon landing, the moon landing on you, but first you must break the soundbarrier popgate, lace up your wingwing shoes and lower the cockpit glass and take off after me fast on grey runway tongue of Destroyer and join the military-incestrial complex consciously you already are a part of by paying the taxes you do to kill people you don't know who don't look like you and since you can't recognize your own feelings anymore, how can you recognize the right of others to exist with different clothing on? This is an outrage but it is gently the moon landing on you in moonboots, your surface cold silver dusty and the drifting sands go all over your face and bury you in the topsoil of the quicksand fracas fundraiser Grace threw when she renamed you Frank Throne so you could begin a new career as a red mussel stew slurped up by guests imitating the ancient gestures of friendship, long extinct since us all being enemies to each other became necessary to survival of the Punic War Revival Stratagem started by the burnt Papageno in his parrot cage when his beloved Papagenome flew away to imitate other words from teachers he barely knew but was attracted to due to their tenure wallpaper of honors and diplomas used to plaster over the redbrick walls with faces appearing and crying in them as the brick and mortar sandwich comes undone, and revellers turn to the fun of undressing and the wingwing sandal buckles are undone and you're already in it or are it, and there's nothing to explain to anyone: that's the fun itself: the lack of explanation, a zero gravity amvironment.

.   .   ..

JEUDI DA SENSORIUM RUM

Today at 4:27 PM

Ou est le Occupy Biblioteque? This is the Queer Section. Where do you want your book? Fuck it, I've sucked enough glorious pink teen and middle-aged professor cock in this life to earn my place in the Gay Poetry Remainder Container, maintenant. I remember each late boy I kissed but not every man. It's not that you get older, you go numb, and what can we do with that at this louchely temporary space camp. The extra hour is huge. I think that arrow is a marketing tool. The Scorpio stinger eventually falls off from use, sinks to the bottom of the Hudson where it smokes and dissolves and regenerates itself into a fiery Sagittarius centaurarcher arrow which shoots itself up out of the riverocean confluence into the Rover Attic Cumulonimbus Cirrus Circus in the Citrus Grove Sky with its vapor scones drifting down the assembly line. Are you responsible for the work of taxis? Brooklyn between tendencies. In order to. Encumbent now. Varicose payment. The debt and the neck and the guilliotine nostalgia apology SORRY IS THERE SOMEONE SITTING HERE. Yes, my invisible boyfriend Bitewing. You won't see him until Seabring Street. Initially. But then cut up pastry reigns and you have to get over doing things in the usual border today. Order? It's stable. Oresteia table of human flesh dainties. Train's the documentary you watch. It's no different in Europe it's still pretty bad. I tried to treat depression with a trip to it. Industries—I've participated. You know you don't really need a tortoise. Either that or start my own farm. Yeah, that's actually what my dad is doing, sewing, his own garden, he sends me videos about what foundations are fucked up. I like boots in the winter and my quality of breeding. Cos I hate flats. Ai ai io io. So. I don't remember exactly I remember I woke up on your couch fullyclothed. Do you remember it, I don't know. Friday was great but we drank a bottle of Lysine in ten minutes. Everything got a little bit weird after Peter arrived people started having sex in front of him. I kept forgetting who Peter was every five minutes which was so weird. I'm sorry Peter just thrusted himself upon you. No, I don't think he did. How is it? It tastes like beechnut. How do you make almond milk. Tout les matins du mond. All mond, all world champion, champignon mushrooms, and I am a mushroom, and what comes out of me is mushroom. There's no mushroom base lamp. At the office I stay late, seated, I wait for myself to come back from the copulation cubicle, I sit on my own lap, a contortionist. My building is turning into a newspaper stand, so I'm confident my recyclables are actually being recycled. Also, I found out I was going to the gym, and Lyndon B Johnson is standing in my usual elliptical exercise place. I freaked out, tried not to be obvious about it. I, actually I didn't say anything, I was so embarrassed with how I was acting. Weights. I realized there are mirrors: I turned around to have my reaction and I realized: there are mirrors in which he saw it! This is true. Lyndon Baines Johnson, twelvehundredmillionth president of the Rushmore stone statue states in profile. His cock is blue. He pulled it out to show it to you since you are the queer librarian who placed your debut volume "Strychnine Seas of Piracy Sans Abacus Dowry" in the gay section to define yourself with pride and now you are harrassed by the dilating shadow of the oval office as your own anus dilates with a wobble as you introduce the well-lubricated bisexual chandelier into it, or one golden lightbulb frond of it at least,

                                            chandeliers are hanging vegetation, and so I insist, you are my guest and must map it, your erogenous zone, the one remaining one, between your thighs but not the cock, but not the thighs or anus either, the aether rag pressed to your mouth, no, that's magnesium you dripped in your left receiving hand and spread on the back of your neck where the spinal cord joins the head to stimulate secret traffic all up and down the back, the vertebrae train, the Orient Express that passes through Belgrade, where you stay when in the Balkans on Business, leisure, or to meet the tigers at Belgrade Fortress Zoological Garden with your cousin Wolfman, the louche flammable absinthe in your shotglasses come evening, come evening, evening come, come on my face and leave me disgraced at the base of the Terrace Knave Fountain, my bluejeans down around my ankles, are those Levis, are they real or pirated, or is all denim a kind of motley patchwork of spinal cord bar chords strummed by the invisible boyfriend guitar player who plays my spine and is kind of a universal invisible boyfriend, a sog industry, for all those who need to be lonely to drink the wine offered by life from the cracks in the grey fountain marble base, I guess he blew my head off and held me tight and whispered "Sauvignon Blanc" as my grapes went blight. The whole family got together and started yelling about stuff they agree about. It's cathartic. It is cathartic. A white wine will wake you up. A red will make you wake up December twentyeighth in Paris, so it makes Seinse. In making that kind of psycho you have to take shots. Tequila was the first thing and from then I formed the temperance union in my all invited three story starched stiff party jeans. My dad was this total strange hippy person, counting. We forgot Cleveland at the coffee. I'm second oldest actually. I mean three people are not a ghost organized but I am actually waiting and once I'm done what a viscous experience the lava must have, let's interview it at the caldera ridge with all our balding pates singed red for Yorrick sled skull racing down the fresh wet obsidian slope steeper than the vertical cliff face of Fantasm soda machine fountain—O Filou—orange head of plague defenestration stratagem backfiring on you, you have to show mercy to yourself and you're smashing glasses on the floor and dancing on top of the bar and you're dancing as fast as you can, aren't you, little twistbraid of grapes, Fasterbean Damages, Jackanapes and inheritor of mouthfulls of hot load semen spilling from the corners of your mouth to make the coroner jolly and even and calm enough to wake you up with his formaldehyde sponge and paintbucket of jessum. Jessup? Jesso? The canvas priming agent? I applied to be a catsitter. Whatever. I can't be allergic forever. I'm willing a hypoallergenic system into my skin and no one can stop me not even the laws of physics of the lineament-sensitive Milky Way Galaxy. So I get my tutoring clients to come sit on my face until the timer rings and then we play speedchess until replacements come from the wings. My partner sits on me until my boyfriend comes and my husband my wife my sidereal property noise is Phantom's poise as he climbs down from the Paris Opera attic. There are some people who've made it their life. They charge a thousand dollars an hour to teach. Who has that kind of money? You'd think. Genociders grow rich with it and slurp the fermenting cider off their fisting fists. Hornographic, or rather, Hauntographic. I'm a Hauntographer when I'm at it, Attic.

.   .   ..

VENDREDI SAMADHI STARRING SANDRA DEE

Lactose! That's the word I couldn't remember yesterday. Lack dose. The lactose-sensitive Milky Way Galaxy, the autoimmune universe of our selfreflection vanity. Ooh it's hard today:

ON FUCKING REALITY

Librarytime. Mentallydivide. Are you guys working together? Scorpiotime—as if it could be reduced down to that and if it could—merry wet dreams to you the Prince Plinth Filip shin splints of Denmark—heir to the royal statehood grapecluster chandelier shedding bisexual light on the proceedings below, the coronation of Cell Cleo the Echo. Catmorrow.

When I lost Sonny the dog it was a cocker spaniel clock I lost there on my life. I just was a primary fomentor without him I heard his leash bejangling my park thoughts of perambulatory persimmon lehrstuck, I'm stuck on it, what's the script, and then the One Bus flits by and a frog lariat-tongues it down his throat—King Frog John the former seagoat now evolved into Bemindfullness Proceedings. The mindfulnafs buzz in with blue uncertain windowfail light, don't be shy about it, wanting to have fun, even among the graves fresh dug, joy is a survival tool too, Citizen Jouissance must not be forsaken, it's just like when we play Life. Time Life, he's dating countless bedarvellings of Iced Coffee, he's I I I, glass eyeballs jangling in the Diet Coke for softer feelings and lose weight diet pill Dexedrine carbonation like in the Sixties when I never was alive but was so there at that party when they chopped up the grizzly bear Elizabethan Times. The Elizabethans had a heartier humor than we and showed it by funky idiOMsyncretic spelling bee— I'm here, it's been just fun, I'm here to lose friendships and gain them and repair them and it's friendship spectrum no significance, how can I befriend the blank cave wall for eleven years before a friend comes, finds me, chops his arm off as an entrance gesture, a gift for one whose eyeballs are gone now, given to the vulture who just swooped in and ate my spaniel cocker Sonny the dog, he of many names: Dog the

Dog, Cruiser Bruiser—we can talk more after perception frays us flays us in its phrases and we mindfully pray before the kindness takeover of onetwothreefour companies begins and begets itself—of course it's annoying to hear others speak of mindfullness—every one DOES do it their own way—a different angleglade of light projected from the incandescent eyes surfacing from the red wine decanter to see the sky for the first time through the glass the grape makes to shine from its Dionysian forge lights of topsoil prime South Mouth France and Napa Grappa grapesmear pants and then the mannerists close in and poke out your eyes with their prepared brushes—Where is your luster now, Gloucester, Mass? Alabaster Sonny the dog had many names to hide in the fog of: Charlie Brown! He liked that one he would jump up and down and the best thing was when I was alone in the house my parents finally gone to businesstrip heaven on a plane of Ambien and I make spaghetti with Marijuana Marinara a-splattering the ceiling redmap red and I would blast BABA O'REILLY by The Who on the family Pioneer stereo and run around the house, Sonny chasing me in a circle because he is a spaniel and knows I am a bird and has the soft bite to bring the bird home to the hunter's hand, tho I'm no hunter, I'm the fasterbean bird trolley in thick eyeglasses for reading the red ceiling soda splatter map and knowing the way to the movieroom to eat spaghetti with Sonny and watch World War Two bridges go boomboom on the TVscreen courtesy of Steven Spielbird feeding on history as if it were a corpse and not a thing you find out now as it is, blonde with jowls, a Sonny cowdog shepherd buried in the backyard and I go back there with swishing whiskey bottle and sprinkle the gold on his fresh grave and then walk out there again with my brother and he starts crying and my father yells from the porch Don't cry, Son! And I tell him Shut up! this is mindful binding tearing itself apart—the flesh from the dog goes off and the fur from the hand—the paw from the land--we are Huntresses and no one can separate us from Dogland that's why I go tromping through le monde bond pond wandsticktwig wig of straw and iceberries thaw and the dog visits in sleeptime it's not a dream there is no REMing it's visiting time and there's no consolation for losing the blonde bellyrub time of the spaniel spanielling on now in other spaniellands beyond your hand where no leashes will ever touch his neck again he can run the soccer field off the earth he can pick up that whole green turf in his jaws and throw it into outer space so the planets can play soccer with asteroids kicking them through nebula gas goalposts for a point and the Sonnydog paws can bury me in the backyard and he can visit me and pour whiskey, when, now and now, and it will is, and is now is not, is trick or treat and candyblob jawbreaker funteeth, is a minute, the dog hair shed and the serpenteagle flown forth from it, the eyeducts raw from so much crying. My parents didn't even tell me Sonny had died until three days after it happened. My father had already buried him in an allnight hardshovel in the icyground February session. I wanted to be with Sonny when he died. He howled and fell asleep on the library floorforever. What is mindfullness. The dog is off the leash and in the park and I stir my limbs into the spaghetti, the leprosy confetti parade is on, and my skinstrips are peeling off my facemask all by themselves, no need to help them, the barrier between places especially thin when you know they, the departed dogs, never left, there's a whole chorus of them in the front yard and two kids ring the doorbell and leave a small bird skeleton on your front doorstep mat and run off, back into the dark, and you wonder if it's a sign, it's a bluebird corpse, not carcass, it's a real living bluebird skeleton barrette you can hold your hair back with when the bangs get Octoberlong and garish and ashempathic.

.   .   ..

THE FUNERAL MIME SPEAKS FROM THE ASTEROID CHIRON

OB1 WAN THRENODY

The Uncle is dead who left you the gift of elegizing him. You are dubious to do so. Why would you want to continue? Continents steal out from under your feet, stuff tectonic breakage down your sneakers. Your reputation trembles in the talons of the hawk taking you away to Valence Nest Hideaway. See you there if you make it a day or make a day of it or maybe we could get a drink if you've fallen off the wagon yet or if I have or maybe there is no wagon and private anesthesia is all we have left between our meetings, the secret drugs we inhale when our lungs flock south in advance of snowbird traffic, droning the confederate monuments below with our tears, sweatdrops, and shed orange beaks. You are crows now and I am a puffin catapulted from the Arctic circle to the Key West target coffeeshop. I would sit here all day but the sanding machine next door makes bad vibrations and it's not very prompt to be late to the first day of birth at the chemical weapons plant on the window sill of the oval office where I intern as plant waterer and make sure the hibiscus is watered. No that is called the rose of Sharon, the lily of the valleys, the rose of Chiron, the pill-popping of the binder clouds eating up the election tallies of paper. Those hanging chads will make a dapper necktie when they are stapled all together. Why, I salivate upon entering the stationary stores of Monday afternoon, post coffee klatsch, at the scent of September school glue for safety precautions where the inhaling infant mind is concerned. A whole nation of infantilized sloths gobble up couches sofas and divans, not knowing the difference, just so we can learn again to stand.

To stand ourselves and then each other, if it even goes in that order. What order? Chaos border hoarder out of office. Defenestrate it, the wigrack antenna, and the rest of the golden office furniture will follow, out the window in a cascading orange monochrome rainbow.

Excorcism marrow.

POSTHUMOUS PUBERTY PROTEIN POWDER

It's under the horizon but I can see through the earth. Not with X-ray vision, but the original Roentgen buzzing in my head as my limbs drift downstream in their new disjecta membra phase, posthumous puberty. By the time Thor gets into your third house with his hammer and lightningbolt tongs, be ready to renovate your architecture of everyday activities. If only the everyday existed! It's only now that each iteration of it has a unique architectural cheesemelt future—schwing! Wayne and Barthes had their eye on me, but I escaped the Camera Lucida lecture with my cuneiform decoder ring. Now I'm vanishing into a consideration of what happens when Jupiter enters the fuchsia envalanced portals of Scorpio and rends them in twain, and shreds them, as you, kneeling devotee, bow deeply before the sacrificial banana at LONDON 360 TOWNHOUSE, waiting for a tap on the back from the master, Ashes, and afterlife sex in the agora of Chelsea. But you get up and walk away quickly. Did anybody see you?

It's one hundred pounds of his package battering at my head through the bardo curtain cut in half by Jupiter's plunge into Scorpionic wellwater. Knock knock. Well drinks on sale at happy hour flood forth from the Virgola Bar and the sidewalk shed is electrocuted while I practice my loveglances inside it at passing strangers running from possible friendship. My glare is not only not welcoming, it is eel wilkommen. The mauve neon tubes and landscape painter's palette are to be mixed with tongs and moxie and fullmoon drumcircle drums. The mushrooms, you took too many of them, are diluted in your bloodstream with the ingestion of sugar, and you come back down with a Snickers bar by the pool table in the coed House of

Defiance foyer. Who are you waiting for? That friend who fled for California. No, that friend. That friend who fled for California after Nine Eleven. No, that one. No, that. No. N—

VIRGO TO THE TWO PISCEANS

I'm having naughty thoughts: I want a sleepover party with just the three of us. I wonder if the shades are down in the coffeeshop to not give potential shooters a clear shot. It's the day after Halloween. Josie has many times then a whirlpool to be diminished Greek thought paper student. Rapiertongued conversation, come in. Beyond that though is. My back is to the window of the coffeeshop so the shooters will get me first if they drop by the cube of light Corfu coffee shop La Colombe, depending on how many war hours, right here, Brasserie Mozart, Lafayette Avenue and Fourth Street. Sit in the corner all day till you can hear student feet translate the Odyssey for you from the original Greek. I definitely want to do, with my Grandma too, a podcast. That she's dead is only just an inconvenience. I'm in my third and first house at once right now. I also want to record it and immortalize it for myself. I want to know my grandparent Salt. Yours ever, Salt Shortage the Younger. I love my young membrane: we have the archives. The shame. It's just a bigger file so it's still blurry. The cheese is ready to go. Do my Yugo Ancestors go to it? Also these cheermittens are my favorite thing. Seasonal defective association disrober of the hardest order, come in. He looks shy. Come in. Oh I have a dope one of you guys together: photographomania in the entrails we suffered. I had a bunch of Greek tourguides I called them all Orpheus in the cabbage bed. This is not a video game, Author, pay attention.

I know. I want more time there. When I went upstairs to 5c where the fire alarm was chirping I bled out of my finger to get that thing down from the ceiling. Finally now it's silent except in my mind. Excuse me do you think I could squeeze in. No worries. Now worries. Will we get run over in the street by the passing makeshift instantaneous hearses of the minute.

I like how you are silent sometimes it makes me feel like America's wedding girl. The bareness of your ankles. Muscle built till two weeks ago. Even August worried about her paces. If you find someone so quickly, this is then as a friend, I hope you are looking at me for to bed me, have children across from me in the neighboring apartment. I make such a fuss for Reason itself to throw eyeliner tubes at me. I want to be told to make up my eyes and besexy my look at you because I, a muse myself, couldn't comprehend how he makes me feel: you're so deserving of love, all of us. Like, he GETS life, I don't know how. When he first introduced himself we found out the spirit. HAZ TAC truck red with siren blaring by. Everybody so on edge after yesterday eight bicyclists murdered by psychotic SUV driver. What is HAZ TAC? Am I sposed to write a dissertation on signage now? No thanks! I only am time to love. But if so then life is us meeting and asking each other honestly in what ways we are curious about each other and if it includes undressing beyond undressing with the eyes we already do which is unsatisfying after two and a half years of doing it.

I'm almost 3 years sober now without one AA meeting which means I'm in danger of relapse anydaynow. Relapsetop signed me up for a Pelates class so as to dissuade me. Yeah, you seem, like, lighter than Step Two. Gender as sonic violence. The fire alarm bleeds from the ceiling above us. You have to perfect the art of listening by not listening. You are expected to listen to your abuser. But the root of compassion says You have to be compassionate to yourself first if your compassion will evolve real outward and warming to the ones who need it and don't abuse you to deserve it.

Your abuser lover is coming to town in three weeks. What are you going to. Avoid him. If he gives chase. Avoid. Avid avoidance flight pattern fugue state eyelashes. I thought I was a comminicator but. I'm cement and a hangingman hatching in a Haz Tac suit fresh from the egg of wet cement sidewalk. Who deserves to be listened to. And it's not negative it's just digging deeper into. I think it's confrontational in a helpful way. I think you're confrontational in my pants in a constructive bender way genitally sensitive to me and my congenitally clumsy seductionways. I would rather do nothing than tell you I love you I've been rejected so long. And it's also about how I've been polite: you suggested I could break into 5c and take out the chirping smoke alarm. I did it and bled from the finger as consequence. Masculine tear gas private sphere. You didn't want to help me find a bandage. You slept in bed. You woke up only when I cried: I can't find the Band-Aids in the top of your backpack. In this way I learned how it feels to be a Veteran returning from the Trojan War and ignored when I ask for fresh wound dressing.

Insistence on an audience is a male entitlement psychosis. That's why I perform for one mouse to cure myself. Yesterday in the used record store: the owl computer mouse, ha ha, on its mouse pad. I wonder if I will be shot on the walk home through trick or treaters or will the protective Sowin ancestors save me with their Celtic Balkan shield bagpipes no bullet can penetrate.

Halloween. Used to be my favorite holiday. I only want to touch you it's such a rush and to be with the two of you touching each other is the only cure for me I visualize it and it's happening. Let's see us three.

THE SINKING OF THE TECTONIC

the boat moves
the water moves
the shore moves too
the mountains are walking
tectonically talking
nothing doesn't move
we're just all different speeds aren't we
or are we out
not likely to survive
the mass murder we continue to perpetrate
in the name of
bingewatching the shore
to see how it moves
from episode to episode of
alluvial mud movies

.. ..

BLOCK FLUENCY. Kicked out of English. Egg. Eggless. Waiting all day to say it and now that I can I'm sores inside the swords inside. It's painful to not think and the sacrum has its own ideas about prose, poetry, poetry disguised as prose, angry, Sunday night bleak hackward sham. No effort and effort at watering the seeds that say: "Hey, at least I'm not mad like I was that time." What stops me from THANK YOU right effort THANK YOU. What stops me from effort at all? Effort and Grief and what do you call it? Deathbeatific greetings. What stops my efforting madness? Thank you let's start again. Be gentle and specific this time. Laziness. Loungertrauerspiel in kind.

Feeling the fire in the gut now from the ginger.
Linger, gin. Water the seeds of the good mood feelings, like the air-fresheners spitting at timed intervals above the heads of

        shoppers at my favorite zen temple, Whole Foods. There the class war is choreographed to perfection. Put the mute in the trumpet for that sweet sadness sound, or try the orange plunger-mute-cap worn by the non-president. Will he bomb North Korea? The question in subtitles running across everybody's chest. But this is not a timeless question, so it will not survive the severe tests of time needed to enshrine the most immortal poetry. Yet the canon will survive in nuclear-bomb-proof bunkers with my hard drives inside for the aliens to open up and find evidence of what it was like to be specifically alive while the deities got their hair cuts and people gathered around to shoot them with their phone cameras. The poet's scroll is a funerary spaceship shot out into the darkest ether beyond the moon, past the gas giants, into asteroid fields we can't yet see where our mother and sister are waiting to plant a tree on each asteroid headed to earth to teach us not to kill the trees if we like oxygen. Breathing. Efforted that with the lungs, through the pain of gut sacrum mind bleating like the sheep with iron fleece. Iron fleece, where have you gone, iron fleece?

THE NECROPHILE TOURGUIDE

This is George Washington Longfellow's house, this yellow one on the right with the columns. This is my pile of dirt. Will you know how to get back to Harvard Square, Filou? Yes, I have excellent spacial software, else I would try to get lost here and make love with you upon this very pile of dirt, with a floating *trompe l'oeil* painting on each side of us to shield us from the Policemen of Cambridge Snoop Snoop Patrol. *Patois*: I wish I could speak a special kind with you right now, and we could get tight on some homemade Riesling from your backyard, which I've been growing there for months since I was sixteen years old. Speed: that's suddenly very necessary: it means: to keep going. That was a four caboose train and where is it going? Acephallic choo choo,

you know I ride inside of you. The sleeper car is ready for me to pilot you to the nearest star, and I don't mean Alpha Centauri, but rather the Friendship Nebula: the whole of spiritual life NO MERIT NO SIGNIFICANCE is spiritual friends, which does not mean you depend on them for approval, but for mutual support in the practice of spoken candor, to get the truth out. But soft you now, the fair Baristaphilia. Nymph, let us make our cemetery guest gazelle visit, to throw one shovelfull of dirt over our shoulders and, flapflap, masterfully fly away before we are noticed and scanned by the undertaker necrophile swinging his rubber sex toy lantern at all those dissolving larynxes underearth:

"I will love you all now," he says, "and you will give me GLUG GLUG the head I so richly deserved while you were taking off into pupward mobility, and I was left bereft, without a lover, save for these soft limestone headstones oozing suntan lotion SPF 35 for a strong sunblock, as the shovel gulls flap away into the Florida Keys Migration Windstream to download their streaming videos through their orange beaks and dream, carried aloft by halcyon winds way past the hayloft pillow farm earth, scorched by famine and the cricket infestation of locusts awakening from the two thousand year subgrass hibernation to chirp chirp chirrup the stirrups off the horse who shakes with fright at such an overpopulation of winged twentytwenty vision mice. Oh search! Search on, Search Engine, thou'll't never find me in this camoflauge of family words, these bent orange sheds slide off the president's head when he is defenestrated even now, that's what I like about consciousness. Flying needle. Cow of four stomachs and a branch of government in each of them dissolving—solving—ving—ing—v. Flock of shovel gulls swoop off to the south to sing the hurricane to sleep fitfully."

Wait! I haven't told you my visions yet and gravity pulls me down into B-side collection tapedeck oubliette: prison underground where the tears can be found that are the only writing implements now irrigating the ground for the friendly fargone September cornmaze crop. The Halloween Sawvein Cornmaze kid event is cancelled this year due to drout conditions and investment weather taking precedence, the market more important than the climate i'th'short term, so burn it down and build it up again on the banks of the Charles river. The blueblack
water parls parlays and parls and purrs and snarles and chatterbox talks its way back into that Mass memory impeded only by the pain you feel now on the way back to

Uncle Dragon Deathmemo Nebula, the gaseous cloud of poisonous and yet vaccinelike grieflove that keeps sticking its needle into your arm as if to immunize you against death and yet it can't!

And yet the Charles says you get horny for girlsandboys and refuse to distinguish between them. The blue curtains don't. At the confluence of the Hudson and Danube rivers I grow up on a suntanning raft space station for junior grafters learning how to turn a con from the wavelets and salmon spawning therein. I don't buy the waves, I just read them. One tells me how it feels in the body to be attracted.

I'll read two more. Thank you again to the curators of zentangled family shoelaces. The genetics of the situation cannot be properly attenuated or probingly genuflected at by the Cowardly Lion in me, so I return to Pace Mater Saturn to tapdance on the ringispiel until one of its horses, a bay stallion, carries me off through the asteroid belt and back to my family castle, Jupiter, and the long rope bridge between the gas giants and Mars, my orange home barge where I fish for orange fish during Cazimi season, when Mercury takes a dip in the sun and emerges refreshed from the Flame's address to the graves at Gettysburg. How I loved Abe Sunset best but then he disappeared to his eternal home rest. Before there were rest homes there were families the elders were an integral part of. The grandparents blessed the treeswing. We could hear their lovecries long down the pajamasleeve hallways of the evening and deep in the silversteel manuscript scrolltube cannisters. I leapt out of the airplane to get one such tube back from the gluttonwind, and guided myself back into the plane with the help of the Dadda Sonny Controltower

Trinity Voiceover Goiter speaking from the neck of the friendly lucky saltimbanque wind from Rilke Heaven's Wellspoken Deliverance Guardian Oxygen. Oxygeneia to Taurus went, and there anointed the wounded and let them back out into the world to tell the tale of healing well in the salubriously *brchki* birchy wavewaters of the cavern of bubblebaths without bats to charge cover. I even wanted to be pigeontoed in Boston but did not dare there were so many who did it naturally there.

UNCLE LUNGS

Judgy is a problem. Judgy is not where you want to be this holiday season. Have an emotion. No, you have one. I will visit you at Greenwood Cemetery if you visit me in Vanilla Seminary at Valhalla Drive, the home of my sister vikings. Listen, it could be twelve hours or twentyfour years from now. What is essential? My father goes to a ski trip in California for Mercury Retrograde and leaves his bathrobe on the turned on space heater. It does not turn me on. It makes my mother his babysitter. You will be separated from every one you love. Not loving one or one or one is not an option. Love is reality and there is no outside to it, only violent delusion within its circle. Real evil exists in the world and will not exit until we do, the exit wound. The exit wound *what*? Reject! No: every one who auditioned will play a part in the Nativity Play. I'm second lobster, no, I am. But you don't fit with my reindeer antler plan. Well, if you need to be impaled on something, that's a good way to go, Penis-hands of the Apennine Mountains (the app of nine mountains.) What a cool thing to say for La Guerre, (men only wish war was feminine La to get them out of the responsibility for endless deathstruction,) investments proud as shit, electives forgotten, school resumed—a good lawyer is worth his salt in God. I can't listen to this racist South African drug dealer anymore. So don't: tune your attention to your hara two inches below your navel and apply yourself scrupulously to the eggshaped hot buttercluster melting into the top of your head, the crown chakra defiant yet willing to receive the healing of the hot hot hot hot hot wellscented butter egg, a verified traffic-clearing vehichle from Heaven, Massachusetts between Houston and Prince. The wider sangha appears in its cameo formations. Amen. And Amen to the wonderful bandana for smuggling Samedi diamonds in. For the end of the week-

End

Is nigh

Even as it rises to its peak on Saturday Night.

One more Saturday Night. Playing on a Saturday Night

A Saturn ring tambourine.

I don't get high anymore I am high.

My classmates ask me what drugs I took to look with my ears and listen with the eyes the peacock loaned me for Surveillance Tailfan Weekend. Oxygen. In. Out. Thank you, Lungs. Uncle Dragon doesn't have you anymore, but I do for the moment, and he teaches me how prescient you are.

JOB INTERVIEW WITH MAKER

Where do you see your self in five billion years?

I see my self retiring to the eardrum raft, constant change of staff, that would have to be one big eardrum extracted from the Giant by Jack and where has Jack gone? Back to San Francisco. When I arrived Jack would not look at me. I'm sizzled, struck, motherfucked with lust from the eyeglance arrows shot from my comrades' eyeballs and I'm here to tell you about the dear love of comrades, subbing for Whitman today, of course I'm a sub. Subcontracters contracted. Yesterday at the long red room roundtable stage set for THE LAST JEALOUSY OF FEVER, a play by Billy the Kid Yeats Femur Bone. Sounds really fun to teach: I had the youngest dream, oldest crossbow, this person is going to red school. The red studio will speak to the table and grant it wings which grow from the grain of the wooden table hiding under the red table cloth. Deep inside the blood orange chamber we speak and our speech acts are songs and our songs don't speak, they strip you of your bandages, t-shirts, underwears—*unterwasche schneiders von zeitschriftgeistglass schlacht*—shave your brave winter face of icy field stubble. Upon studying the frozen pond ceiling I aced the pop quiz. That chandelier with sassy hats hit on me when I came in,

the twins that applied the same year got into Turtle. You can bring a friend. I won't be it. You, neither of you, returned my email though it was very friendly. The bunkbed is not handy to reach, still in boxes and ready for assembly, it doesn't care if you assemble it or not. The bunkbed exists only as parts, is not sentient yet, is it?

You departed and already arrived at that place where you are one x-ray year or two away from being a nonbunkbed nonhuman. SHOW ME YOUR FACE BEFORE YOUR FIRST ANCESTOR WAS BORN A HORN ON A UNICORN IN THE MEDIEVAL TAPESTRY OF SHORES USED TO WRAP UP SINGED BROCCOLI TAPAS. To fill up and drink the vodka, pour it into a

stomach sponge. It's funny, better than stinging nettles, it's viper percent, no presh! Presh is short for pressure. Did you text me back, Terrence Paradise? Will you come to the Butler talk tonight? Did you work today? Yes. What time do you get off? Tetanus. Department of Movement. I was tired but I got that fulltime job the week I turned 26 I moved to Astoria. Between me and my boyfriend I have a wedding tree of three dogs one cat and one drummer, he certainly is a white marble sarcophagus stolen from the Met. Met is Metropolitan Museum of—

You know abbreviations mean death. When I get off work I have to go right home and get off. My phone died this year. Are you thinking of another adoption. Not for a long time. Yup. That's what we the people do with our time, homework, even if it means scissoring fingers off our betters, our bosses, our revenge fantasy phantoms, and we take each finger and attach it to a necklace we wear to the coffeeshop. Nobody notices while you are babysitting that cat.

I wash, just washing up from watching Chester's cat. It was a mean cat and exuded dead cat smell. I want to bathe in that. I was brave enough to let it die on my watch. Cat-sitting is the only place I can get some reading done.

That's when we meet in the blood orange room. The pulp in our mouths feels like a chandelier of electric candles crunching in our teeth. Do you like the new comrades. They're nice. Every year they get more and more like snowflakes. Everybody does disorder as much as a dad center for anything centaur-related like when the student kills the teacher by dropping an envenomed arrow on the teacher's foot. No! It is a hoof. The hoof splits even farther apart than it already is—

Cloven is the word. But the teacher invited the student. Correct or Incorrect. But the teacher invented the venom the student fills him with through seeming accident. The teacher, too weak to suicide himself out of the sublimation life, sets up the possible scenario for accidental professorcide. The teacher was a centaur, the student a marine, and where they go together now nobody's ever seen.

ANASAMADHI PATHOLOGY

So there it is, Sister Ister, the same wound flows. The Ister is a river Holderlin addressed, but I don't know it. I just flow with the typos. Sunday with the Insane: the typo of Ister for Sister carries me away, gored on its rhino horn. Rhinos and Typos are long extinct. Enough sad song. Reach back for your pillow. It will go slow today because everything is underwater, hostage to the glow, you wait to cross the street, Eleventh, with a microphone in your belly and holding two bags of laundry from Holderlinear Time Laundromat. At the Dove Coffeeshop people save seats with their bags. We get to sing to each other. A beautiful bespectacled trans woman, a woman, with dark red dyed hair, laughs in the cafe and I wish I could be with her, she drowns out all the job interview talk and I can hear myself move again. Mauve moan. L'aube. L'aube, daub me now with your fierce tears, I pray to the sweating crayon spine located in my back between my shoulder blades and way down there where I can't see or won't: I've forgotten my genitals so they forget me. It is impossible to enjoy something if there is no ease. Hence I am a born bottom. But no one will ever take me up on that just now. Most often I feel attracted to the mentally still because I myself have triceratops disorder, extinctiveness with trapezoid tendencies. My third horn comes out of my third eye and defends me against the T Rex: Memory. I was more into Queen because I am a big queen, not a dinosaur, but a Freddy Mercury lover. OH MOTHER MERCURY SEE WHAT THEY'VE DONE TO ME, I CANNOT RUN I CANNOT HIIIIIIDE. With these lyrics Freddie Mercury gives birth to himself with the Doula Wand. He didn't need permission, he created it, as I don't need lyric permissions to quote poplar songs from the time I was born. 1985. No. 1975. That makes me 42. Which is a 6. I'm in my devil year, is it worth it to say this and risk a curse, I'm cursed enough as it is: triceratropic impotence. It seems you would like to make some changes. Wouldn't it be nice if we were boulders, then we could roll down hill and crash into each other at bottom. I feel to the bottom born—

I need a boyfriend who will abduct me and take me to Paris and dump me when I ask but only then: I have to unleash my fantasies or they will unleash me from the earth, comet-like. Would I like to be a comet? If I'm not already please kiss me, the suspense is unpleasant, a leaky blue pen in my left breast pocket, what is all this world, I mean are you back yet, are you ever coming back? Don't get up I'm only shaving my head, I interrupt myself best when I listen to you, change my direction without losing the breathwindcircus, because the breath is not fixed, Mutable Kid, Amputee Mandate, come out of the tent. SUNDAY WITH THE INSANE, I call my carpentry class, the students call it a workshop, but they don't do the reading, there is none, live! Kiss yourself in the mirror if you don't know: the looking glass looks back at you and flirts: from its opening medicine cabinet I breathe in the dust of the gathered ingredients, of meds: Aspirin, Band-Aid, Neosporin, Lifestyle ultra thin lubricated luncheon condoms glow in the dark wintermint spark—for the tonsils—if you still have them—hunger with their library alcoves open for tiny students playing gems in the school play: emerald, rhinestone, lapis, as the day is batshit lapidary in its untowardly todayness anus third eye which looses the gaseous enlightenment clone called delusion lion into the constellations of the Forehead Nebula painted in gold and soon to be towed for parking in a no spaceship zone.

So there it is, Sister Ister, the name wound flows —

this is not Solaris, but to do the thing I want to do most, travel, you need four-Lear-clover honey, most wealthy Americans are one half enriched uranium already, that is true, for my father's house has many McMansions, and a jetting suicide icecream cone spiked with cyanide, and to travel maybe you need it. My coffeeshop neighbor refuses to cover his mouth as he coughs intermittently throughout his coughversation. The mittens of the minute, up to the minute, the Wolfvendor News Service says. I love the idea you can lick friends around the anus without spoiling the friendship: I mean it changes everything: one flight together. Take that part out of every equation and I hate it. My hat shrinks in the wash, and I know you hate hats, but this one's majenta, I can't help it, it matches the aviation valour of the mauve phone my mom bought me for my Jupiter in Virgo birthday three years ago.

My mom now under the snow of a heavier grief than ever: the death of her brother Dragan from lung cancer. I can't, can I, call him Dragon anymore, the codeswitching opiate wears off. My dad's the trustee of the entire family wealth which splintered from hoarding on too long as everything went under during the Freight Recession. My father sat me down and yelled: WHAT ARE YOU GOING TO DO IF I GET CANNED!!? NOT WORK?!! Still the coughing of coffinshop naybor. It's so worth it to risk infection for present dictation, auditory gyzm cumfartable after all. If I have to go die, yes I do, but not yet, but I'm not, you're not getting any, or are you, I can't do Serbia in two days, it's just not even possible, like a weird sense of humor, the present tense of rumor, kids raging like Aspartame Mom, sensitive Dad, he raised them as an iced tea bonus, my coffinshop naybors are my models and I dare not live without their voices, so terrified am I of my own howl-owl-unknown voce fruitvox foxes—

everytime I see them the orange blurs fawn over me during the L'apres midi d'un faune previews, when I watch from the wings, I say it's my fault, when I watch myself basted with formaldehyde in the family vault. I long for vinyl, the Danube Vaultz that twirls through Budapest, Belgrade, to be in the air somewhere, to lose it ocassionally but come back, Coffeeshop Naybors, we're not in Rigormortis, New York, are we, is this embalming fluid we drink daily? I don't believe in the daily Amsterdam, I don't want to say, just die, walk around the shellfish shelves of Small Fry Valley, where the skiiing is nigh. We're on gluten now! And by the way, Nietzsche, you're going to need your Torino horsemane wig now, cos I'm gonna throw my own funeral party, even if I'm a dyed-in-the-wool Marxist, as you most surely see I am by now: the only thesis chord I ever play is this: THE RADISHES OF ALL THE DEAD GENERATIONS TASTE LIKE BRAVERY UPON THE PALETTES OF THE LIVING.

Radish Hardon Garden Arden Bards, thrive on,
Thrive,
Life
Radishes,
Red
And smashed into the eyeballs of
Mump,
The first president to be peacefully removed from office

Via placebo still spring water injection
Presently
Amen

And all will be well again

when you give birth to yourself like Freddie Mercury did—but wait—he died of AIDS when he was barely 45—

the new lifespan of us queer lovers should be 45hundred years alive at least in each other's arms, washing the chloroform off our shoulders to wake each other from the operating theater of the independent shoulderbone who performs surgery all alone and needs no assistants to hand him pliers because this shoulderbone surgeon Self is an American Individual Exceptionalism and not subject to the thaws of physics iceberg.

A neighbor brushes your back with her shoulder bag: this is all the Reiki of the Curd Reich you can take right now: please leave the milkflood of the coffinshop and return to your life in the embalming capital of the globe: Cow York: squeeze my breast and let me lactate, though I'm ostensibly male, though inside I feel the deal fell through, the remaining testosterone fled into the bonfire end of October, "the last nice night of the year," as David Larsen called it last night. Dear friend David Larsen,

I called you Brazil last night, (though David Brazil lives in Berkeley and you are here with us in New York now,) not out of malice, but simply because I want all my friends to be under one fruit tonight, the solar grapefruit midnight sun of mid-November Battery Park—and also my sister Ister lives in Rio de Janeiro, Brazil, and I wish I was with her. She is pregnant now and I would like to help her, bring her her art supplies as she works in the darkroom, or did she stop now, are such sink chemicals harmful to the baby unborn? Ask the unborn!

Unborn, come in, release me from the chloroform trance of the surgeon North of Houston, right around my koshmarkosmos vainface, blood gushing down phonecord childhood trip eyebrow split. Do you need my history to do it? My Balkan ancestors were slaves to the Ottoman empire five centuries and I carry impalement in my DNA like a centaur whose hooves have been amputated by spectral scalpeltoothed surgeonwolves. "You're shaking," my rehearsal mates always tell me when we're making a play. I inherited a tremor from my deceased grandfather Milosh, whose name means: Mercy does me. Do me, Grandpappy Name, incest is just a family treeswing that hits me in the face when I'm not looking and knocks out all my teeth, which I don't need anyway, now that I'm here just for sucking. Prison lucking out to have me. Denmark, New York, Elsinore Whore I am, and I don't charge enough, but only so you'll know I don't need the money, I'm in it for the screwing. Bloody motley motel sheet laundry. Let me take it in and change it in my intestines: that's how the priests read prophecy unravellingly. Tapeworm casette tape body. Thinning hotly. Tongue motley. Toga botfly. Invasion by ship or drone. The world sinks into its winter monochrome and when the bathroom door won't open it's locked, no matter how bad you have to go, dear coffinshop neighbor, pacing before the frosted glass, through which you can barely see me piss in all 52 states of undress, delivering the state of the union address to Twentysixhundred Pennsylvania Avenue. George Washington sailed the Delaware blue icy hues for a painter to capture it with his scalpelflash rabbits glinting off the blade: into the wound with you rabbits of the healing whitebloodcell goo!

TWENTY FOUR HOURS WITH FRANCIS BACON
IN THE CHESTNUT TREE OF HEAVEN

CINNAMON THEREMIN

Chestnut Prism
for those who need to know
his name is a lense
that makes me snow
semen earrings on one
whose branches are
swinging! swinging!

the tree's boyfriend is me

    trim the pubes
    and get ready for the muse

LAVA

Francis I'm lying inside my lava cone thinking about you
my hand reaches down and holds my newly shorn penis
pink and happy and Peter Palace
Nostalgia research only two million light years from
the center of the sun will now go on
in the entrails of my stun gun abdomen
How verklempt I feel to look up and sigh
at your wall of paintings as their cool acrylic drips down on me
I am a snowcrab drifting over your pink nipple islands and
down along your eversolong dancer's pole
Cummings will join us for a threesome in the produce section
I hand you a pink grapefruit half I chopped it
open with my machete
this time I kneel before I want you inside me
to show you what my insides look like so you can
paint them with my entrails
I kneel before you let you gore my throat
I want to paint your erect member with my mouth
that would be a good painting full of silver drips
no one will ever fence in
here we are in the new treehouse to try it
I brought red plain Trojans unlubricated
to suck your latex dong until you fill its reservoir tip with cum
I tongue it I tongue the tip so quick with flicks of
my cooling serpent tongue

FRANCIS BACON CRITIQUES MY PAINTING

lots of snow
of course you are a bottom
look at this cumfest
pastel on wet media sketchbed
are you going to freak out
if I get naked

        no

are you sure

        I'm not going to freak out

and you did get naked
and it was wood

    we embraced
    my pink hood
    against your hoodless head

and that was better than being dead
I've been dead and know

    spindly charcoal lines
    sketch paper flies
    this pink dildo boat you plunge into me now
    I like its rippled head and how you twist it
    in and out of me

I cram all summer for your geology exam
creaming your tentrock formations in my ass
and mouth and
analoralcircuit
        many hazelnut paths we go nuts in

if you were here
you would nut in my mouth
I could spit it out
use it to lubricate you
until you shoot again
into the back of my golden moviehouse organ

my adam's apple is really eve's
no snake no adam
only eve and her
mangosteen
escape the plague

> *the only reason I'm still alive is*
> *I was a top*
> *I am a top*

and I bottom until I can't walk
I want to bleed from down there
a bloodflow staircase of braided drives
if you can't imagine that
you must not be wearing your pink pastel party hat
there I just drew it for you
so you could see how I love you
seriously and yet with total fun
that's just how you feel between my buns
when you do turn me around so forcefully
I see the grecian pyramids you see

I open my vermont bear mouth for you
to throw your slow snowheap into

how do I do it
I don't know
no method porn will show
just how I play host
in the unhome zone

filip fluids flow down coastal balm way
moving due south
drip out my cloacal mouth
puckered from your pink cock crown
sliding in and out as we play
just the tip
you feel in me like a navy ship
charting frozen seas heretofore virgin
and now in need of your stellar surgeon
palette scalpel

      throw acrylic at my navel
      while you creamcheese my loxpink bagel

please don't fear I will push you
I am patient and gentle like you

    when you get naked dressed undress again
    to feel our mutual crucifixion in the 69 position

                storm spume
                pale rails
                ruby whale
                wound paint
     n   a   i   l   s

BETWEEN THE GLOBES

    can I ask you an anatomical question

        sure

    was I inside you

        no you were
        teasing the hole

        can we keep this here
        handy paper bag
        of condoms and lube
        I don't want to do this
        with anyone but you

but I'm so much older than you
in real life I mean

        but we are no thing but in between
        this little intergap
        is so hot to me
        I want you to gape me
        I pull on your bellrope
        and there is no time
            bury your latex nozzle cock
        in my throat
                we are the same age
            teenagers at agon

        don't worry if my front thighs get
        cut against your wooden drawingdesk edge
        I like a little pain and spank me harder please
        you're a born spanker spank

    hornspanker harder please
    masterclassplease

thank you for your wonderful belly
I want you to breathe with it forever

    take care of this you say as you hold my balls and cock
    I will and you take care of this I say
    caressing your whole body I want it forever
    please get younger every time you cum in me
    by the fourteenth spurt you will be a teenager
    and I will be in the infancy of my genius now
    lightning strikes through my body when you look at me

    yet I don't expect anything restrictions breed
    only to see you again and again bamming it into me
    as I turn my back to you and you conglobe me

hey can I I'm not going to go inside I just want
to get between the globes

my prehensile bottom
accepts your pink tile stick freely
and with glow palms on me
now can I rock
freewigs from the wigrack tree shaking
under our tectonic shiftings
and shed silk nightshifts we were never
wearing to begin with !

in the pharmacy cum supermarket
between the aisles no one will see
we have all the condoms we need for free
the aisles creaming with us
oh this must be innisfree
a cabin of clay and waffles made
we will build here and eat it
when we pour our syrup in it
o the microscopic mammoths in the tipdrop precum nylon strand
you catscradle off my dick with your painter's hands
oh divine toe callouses nuzzle against my dick again

so what can I do when I'm pinking in you

I want you to press my face against your wooden
drawingdesk drafting table with the draught
blowing across it from the window
and take me from behind right here in the skylight room
so my scream breaks the skylight
as you cum so hard you shoot me to the top of the blinking
empire state building
and I paint it rainbow with my gay pride dick
tho you say it's not gay I don't know what is it slavic

postmodernism has foreclosed on any soul at all let alone
slavic soul
and that's what I am
and that's what
you can have
I give it to you
chestnut prism zoom

away and back into me
wraith grace
stalactite creaming in me
who's the top
and who's bottom of this cave ceiling

spelunker poker dealer
I love it when you take your shorts down just a little
over your ass
and then you pull them back up
floppy foreskin shorts on your whole dick body
I need chicken
you have to heat it
my whole body feels like an erection
I like your nipples you should pierce them
oh no I would never pierce anything
I was just thinking you could advertise
your hotness to the world
oh I would nevertise I only want you
in the chestnut zone amentone clavier plays itself
that would be eggs up
throw my legs over your shoulders
and plunge your self into the freezer
ready to go as soon as I get home

tectonically orange briefs stripped

my prehensile bottom accepts

.   .   MANHATTAN FRUIT EXCHANGE
              PURVEYORS OF FRUIT & VEGETABLES
              TO THE FINER HOTEL RESTAURANT

chestnut
tree
doctor
            has

            my
conglobular
       vowelglobes
       of
       ass that
he fucks and spanks—
kneading the O—

amen flask of 80 proof roof wrinkles
glittering under the perseid meteor shower

"It's babies"
from his dick
with
purplish
vulva folds
right under the
          ridge

I belong to francis paint
            chestnut
      treedoctor
           heart
director
      I want him to
           cut my thighs
against the edge of
his wooden studio desk
a born spanker
his first
    time
spanking
was me

      images known as 8 o' clock in the morning top me

spyglue applicator snake
sliding in and out of
slide carousel ribcage me

all I want
      a p.h.d. in
           is sucking your cock

                well there you're emeritus

      oh it feels like a bathtub
      oh you can get it that far
      down your throat you should be an opera singer
      my rose reopened in another key

correspondence in heat
correspondence with you is very me

o choral spawndance across my pubic lawn of
innisfree island of clay and bottles made
to break and spin the bottle out of me
with kissing amen and semen my belly
to your belly you pressing your cock into me
drink I want to drink all your cum and then some

let's stop at pathside trench and dig it deeper with our foxhole-probing dicks to end all wars trick to trick to trick and now I need just you jousting inside me I will be your knight of innisfree and also gwinnivere bathing in your spermteam
I mean

    dear francis please tell me it's okay and I can see you again and
dear francis coastalgyzm in me I'm free
I'm so free the tambourinetambourine

.   .   .   .   .

are you sure you don't want to take some condoms home
for your zucchini
yes
I have lube ones at home
but I have to say after you
that zucchini is going to be so inadequate
oh don't forget your other boyfriend
I was literally in heat like my ass

was burning to be entered by you
amen and I guide you in
so you could tease my hole you did
semen and I love your
      "find me where I was before"
scriabin skippingstone lake no shore

    .   .   .   .   .

I don't want any francis but this one

all I want
    a p.h.d. in
   is
sucking yr cock—

          well there you're emeritus

I just want my emeritus chair
to have embedded in its seat
a pink rubber replica of your cock
for me to lube up
and spit on and sit on
while I write you
          emails
         from
     beyond bottom

    .   .   .   .   .

          can I call you

I love it when you call me baby you can call me whatever you want

    it
    threw
    me
        hermeneutical
        wild wisteria
        growing on
            no buildings

   .   .   .   .   .

can I ask you an anatomical question

was I inside you
no you were teasing the hole
I thought I was in the bottom of you
and I thought
should we get you some lube
or maybe you are self lubricating
or maybe you lubed up before you came over
where did you learn to like spanking like this
my parents
ah that's honest

        is that too hard
no it would need to be ten levels higher for it to even hurt
it feels so good
        what does it feel like
electric sparks flying from your hands straight to the tip of my dick

   .   .   .   .   .

he gives me thighmassage
cumcanvas caravanserais of spunk

I have an anatomical
            question
was I actually
            inside you

yes you were teasing the hole
and I let you in yes I did id and all
pink limb
crown
and shaft empire entire
inside me I want
my manvulva amenwagon crashing against your pink wedge and over it and overitoverit until I come through the top of my hilltop crownhead

I'm
so
not
over
it
I
mean
you
every
time
I
think
I
am
you

back into
view
and
spoon
me
on
my
ice
bed
at

18

you might find your thighs
especially erogenous this year

    flesh

shouldn't we get you
some lube I love you francis spill your genes in me
dna staircase semen
   spill it in me I want to drip out your dick
     and fall on the floor
   pleased at last
     prayerfully amen a man at last I go to school here
   someone is digging finally my allegheny serviceberry

it's not sex
making love feels so different

I don't feel dirty qwerty
because I'm piano
keys on your trolley
    yippee

sublimation eventually becomes repression
and that's gluetrap
I need goo
find me where I was

I always travel with nuts
I have a cashe of clothes at this end of the studio
I've just got to get into
I love your gesso white creme fraische pants
with matching creamsicles in each pocket

can you get in love with me a little more vocally
so what if the authorities bust down the door
you have a deadbolt in it
but your live bolt is in me
in this studio we make into a long rectangular bed with no
mattress in it

. . . . .

balkan oral epic
I thought you were talking about
the blowjob you just gave me
oh I was
I was !
hahahaha
I am !

because you were inside me fully orally
to the base

just the tip is no longer just
it is like oh my god just give me all your fuck
fuuuuuuuuuuuuuuuuuuuuuuuuuuuuuuuuck
ck one
give me all your ck one
oh fuck me like a nun monk something antlerovich tennis
player locker room savior of ankles
you even fucked my ankles
you got on me on the creamswivel chair on wheels
and stopped those wheels
and gave me your weight all of it
I tantrically inside came of it

.   .   .   .   .

in case of loss please return to celebration

I have never felt anything as great and wildly late as the pinkpoint of your erection coming up from behind me
and slipping inside me
I love you and there's nothing for it but love
which continues to grow from our fingers
like gloves
a foolish simile--attend!--but let it pass by and go
to innisfree to flower naturally garconning around the sky of j'attend j'arrive

yesterday evening we came for each other first time
blessed blessed event
I want to live in your deportment I'm getting erect saying this
and straddle you on tower queen ice bed
and whisper you're fucking me as you fuck me

your pink crown goes right in and does not come out
the entire night just the tip ship teasing me
I first mate on the just the tip ship d'accord and you mate
me mate with me we have baby splatter all over the ceiling
splatter fellatrix call me

because it is the ultimate ecstasy to have your cock in me
nothing is better than this no woman approaches no
man neither only your paint cleaver stuck in my flesh der
rosencleaver amen

                    guest host fellations

    the next stop is darien

        stand clear
                lear
                      of the gloaming doors

   .   .   .   .   .

                are you okay yes it's just a lot of
blood lots of snow on the rug of my conglobular feelings for
you

there is no burninger honey than this tidal surge when you look at me when I look up at you with your cock in my mouth your crown goes bulbous I feel it flex I forgot just how much I love doing this I know I never loved it as much as this I've never ever done this before I'm a virgin gorge with your deep pulsing thing in the back of my throat its epiglottis bliss schist nonlubricated latex sheath tastes good to me it tastes good to me warm with the throbbing heat of you and your good thingmeat in me I'm sucking as if it is oxygen it is air giving itself to me through your pink cruise tooth spiking me

THROWNNESS DUET

I'm using you

> So
> I'm learning

But is that learning hurting you
How does it feel when you're thrown into your body with it

> I'm using you too
> You're my muse

You're using me

> Yes
> You

because the deer go gathering wild strawberries this time
of fall with baskets on their antlers even so puncture my
chest as if it were a bathroom stall wall
at least I would have a glory hole
through which I could breathe
instead of this whale blowhole
through which I spout rubywoundpaint
did you not love me in the first place

> You dropped your pants
> and you're not the type of guy
> who does that
> not an exhibitionist
> and you were so cute
> and then I saw your ass
> and wanted it
> and by ass I mean everything

Please master spank me
fuck the meat pout of me till there's a
saliva spider chandelier
on my bedroom ceiling illuminating us oh yes amen
buggerfuck me amen master
dungeon fuck me for good like the wet slut boy I am amen
deepthroat pilot pink cockpit throb flex in me and make my mouth your gym

"FOR OCCUPATION—THIS—"

DEAR AUTODEFENESTRATED SELF

who now to flirt with? Many of my friends in university go missing in heroin dormitory and never come back. Missing in Action is a euphemism for blood of the young converted to liquid billionaire sharktank water green with cash and ash couch—

EKONOMIA MIA POW—

a veteran with one hand, the other in the oilconomy sand. The oikos house on fire and who will you rescue the grandfather clock or the grandfather?

or the friends, the parents, the teachers, the kids, the little children

suffer the little children

don't suffer the little children nothing, rescue them, let those proverbs go and verb yourself into the know if you can. If not or if so: both are delusion, cos you don't believe you will die do you? Intellectual maneuver to say you do, but do you feel it with your whole calfskin? Will I be thinking about that then or just pouring hot coffee on my wrist imagining you saying *prima prima* in baby German, German softlanguage baby talk for excellent.

How excellent is it when the wisteria above our heads offers its winding steps to get to the top of it, the redbrick list of incidents, and shall we pause for a spot of research on our phones, Pegasus? Once twenty minutes runs out we can go back to candelabra-making camp and learn how to solder the iron to the very elbow going ahead, out of the body. The third elbow departs from my body in brassy candelabra shadow, and the advanced scout goes ahead of the redwood curtain to see what's ahead, what the unicorn said.

Experience.

When you descended into Zuccotti kiddy pool did the peepee taste like the future you had heard of in your golden shower wet dreams after watching the bluejays mate in the open air aviary of the Ramble Central Park? and you would not stop to be cruised, the plastic bird feeder tubes dangling in branches above. For the birds

it is not a monolog, it is a dialog with the estranged dailies, more important than anger management, and how can you, after all, manage anger when the oikos oink oink economy house is on fire and you must rescue your friends and there is no fire escape and you cannot resucitate, you did not undergo the proper lifeguard CPR training—

the chlorine got to you even at the edge of the pool, chlorine delphine autodefenestrated self, Badger Mammon, how unkind to call yourself thus, and yet how accurate withal. Where do we go to now for recovery— somewhere soft and *prima*?

Premies, the diminutive for premature babies. I'm still *premie* and I just turned fortytwo, but there is no fort can hide my hungry kitty kitty libido whiskers and Milk says spidersilk is a repelling cord I can climb down Dover Zuccotti Cliffside with, to get at the memory tide and wash my cut up feet in it, as I bestride the fault of California Methlab, and board the Earthquakernautica ship that takes me out of the burning earth and flies me on autopilot to the nearest naproom immune system with white bloodcells dissolving into horseshoe nebulas clanking around an unidentified flying iron nail.

    Who threw it? You threw it. Youth. Who's Youth? You with your milktooth still invaginated in the semblance garden with the saliva of the librarian rain dripping down on you and cleansing you of the seasalt accumulated in the cuts you got scaling down the Adriatic cliff into the swim home, long grateful for surviving the inadvisable steep climb down, down,

    down where Gravity can be friend or enemy depending on the tide and how far it pulls you out, and what rock can you jump from at the right angle not to break your third elbow but let it ride out as a bone boat carrying your dead self safe to the other side of the mountain you never knew was there till you climbed it?

GEORGE WASHINGTON PISCES

Repeat after me: I, George Washington...
Pisces...Fishfather of our gills filled with quarters...
I remember Occupy Wall Street, New York chapter,
The Peoples's Library at Zuccotti Park

Rhiannon rings

So much

Friends. But what is the way to Dover? Is that a good cookbook?

Violin practice heals the goiter within a week or your iguana back.

Why would you be symptomatic? Zuccotti Park nostalgia conjugation: it sucks, I sucked, you sucked, we sucked

There.

Wait: when did you break up? This summer, he probably wanted to sound sincere. Then I hooked up with Donut. Tarot Donut. He was still dating that teacher. They were dating? Look at him! Good for them. Yeah, I agree. I feel like he has a really credible job. Does he? I remember that. I remember Zuccotti Park. Social life. Platforming. The accumulation of cultural capital and the clap of poor Tom Snow. Poor Tom's a-cold! RETHROW ME THE FOULFIEND FELLOW. I haven't seen me since. The accumulation of cultural capital and friends and you becoming policemen you will never talk to again. Friends who accuse you of everything they do, but can't see, so they and you can continue to do it. Hey. Nostalgia is a poisonous algae bloom in the Central Park Turtle Pond hippocampus. I remember when friends were buying hats to party at places. At a bar they'll hug you. A greeting and then defenestration.

Friendefenestration. I know that sounds bad, but, what the chaplain, you have to work up your arm strength somehow. The fall season is underway even though heatstroke remains a daily danger in this our autodestruct ecosphere. Oh you are amused by it are you. Thank you for your spiritually constructive memhorror. The author Devon has this really weird selfdeprecating thing with this Tinder fellow right next door. He's me, the resonating hallway thing. Oh we grow so rotund together

we strike flat the thick rotundity o' the world. Rut rut rut rut rut. Glottal Rut. Glottal Hut. Glottal Butt. Slottal Gut. Glottal Mutt. Glottal Shut. Glottal Rut. Glottal Author Smoke after the break in a document house. I'm too embarrassed to say I'm into him because I'm intimidated, but we, like, cuddle a lot. His name is Memhorror. We're engaged. I'm engaged to the National Book Award. Yeah, same.

FROM THE DAYBOOKS OF FASTERBEAN DAMAGES

In speeding up to bypass the censor Politeness I become angry, cheap, unenjoying. How's that? Have I repented enough? Back at it:

Jupiter ingressed into Scorpio just now. Just this
Morning around ninethirty a.m. eastern bandwith time.

Do you notice the changes? And get back to me if you do.

I hope you feel better soon! For I do miss you. What advice could I give you that you have not already packed up in your red on red motley bundle? Have more than thou showest. No more storm rerun. Sunlight keep it going.

Sunlight keep it going.
Sunlight keep it going.
Sunlight come on.

Wear the dishrag. I had dinner with one of my friends. It's so Joycean I want to throw it all out, sub-Joycean of course. Nothers by comparison. Five hours and then obedience school. I feel like we're not in, we are detention. Water retention circus. Bedbugs and sudden infestation of the librarian's apartment. The aliens are strange with their scheduling, and sunflares give us precogs or meta-cogs to be more precise. Are you buried in a cogfin, Uncle Dragon Frienddragon Frienddefenestration OOOMMM. To forget mourning you I study MIDNIGHT IN PARIS and realize puff puff pass alienation. Bong puff drifts upward past the face, the sward of state, and current events of the judgy river Hague. Just go do anything with the demon Mara, even that would beat math homework, sitting under the cold tree all night to give it the warmth of your departed appetite.

I wish I could remember TEMENOS TEMENOS what the trees of Zuccotti Jukebox told to me TEMENOS TEMENOS beer and barley and corn and whiskey and autumn time harvest pantry.

Double double. Depublish the bubble of white supremacy soupfest, depublish, dissolve it even though you know not how, do it anyway, it is impossible sob sob and

Impossibility, I'll see you in like ten minutes

Possibility, thou fairer house than prose, I'll see you in like ten midnights

IMPOSSOBOBOBOBBLE IMPOSSYBIL OF THE CAVE OF CRIES FREEZING INTO RADIATING QUARTZ CHANDELIERS impoissonfish
Impoissonfish
Uncatchable
Yes
Impossibility is the perfect aphrodisiac for you you periferal scribe of impossibility ensemble
Itselfnesses
Myriad
Experiencing
Themselfnesses
Herselfnesses
For the age of Aquarius belongs to the women poets
And now I will shut up and continue. All was ready shrilly whistle belly for the contonuation of le langue voyage.

Covered with rainbow stickers, can I sleep in your laptop? Will you download me? I've been born into the wrong sex but I don't know what it is and there is no right one is the only thing I know. I know it emotionally. I don't know Jacques of Arden Sherwood Forest the Sea of Reeds the Birnam Wood babblethon the forest of old highschool Lake Cochickewick fire trail stolen from the native tribe like everything else on this cursed land.

We the Occupiers taking back the Lenape land on the southern tip of Manhattan as if it were ours. We liberate ourselves of our livers with whiskey and tyrannize each other and all around us the undercovers of the FBI and Occupy Poetry Assembly Night say: Daylight is fired.

You can't be an editor of the Occupy Poetry Anthology. You can only be a facilitator! You say editor, I say facilitator, let's call the whole thing soft in the head, soft boiled brain of a late October heatstroke in these our severely strained strains of late Viennese Hapsburg waltz states. What's the haps. The haps is in the flooded square where the military and sanitation workers cleaned out us occupiers with police sawsles. From Libra to Scorpio the big change is: the breath comes from the genitals not kidneys anymore and we are going south toward feet toward the hour of six o' clock dragon meridian--death and eros intertwine around the medicine tree by the drum circle vibrating Liberty Plaza. The ghosts walk from Ground Zero and into us. We have visitors and don't know who they are. How do we cough this air out of us. It's not air. It's guests. Gusts. Geistguts.

FASTERBEAN DAMAGES

I'd rather not be concerned with this. The continuing adventures of Fasterbean Damages on his way to a recording contract. I cannot cap it yet. I'm just beginning to know it, and need more shows, a whole fall tour, to even begin to inch near the studio and flay down the tracks. Skepticism. Traffic. We'll take a meeting and pour the new coffee into each other's ears to see how really hot it is and if the eardrums can take it. Take it, Fasterbean Damages, take it and head for the out of range of rent hill, there to regroup with an orange tube of rattlesnake pills. His coffee is delicious, though it burns the throat. Whose coffee is it? Corfu's. The big beet-red drunk island man. The proprietor of the Cambridge, Mass bed and breakfast, Swerving House, told me at her reception desk: "There is no more romantic man than the Balkan man," to which her African American receptionist replied "Okay, I'll take your word for it." I should kill myself for this tragic accident of being born a man, or being able to pass for one, though I am owl-salamander by spectrum. You might call this evasive, but I'm not, I'm situated with all of you on the Cusp of Magic, and I too was abused by my Mother, Father, and Brother, the holy trinity, as when corn pancakes are served after the latest show of Fasterbean Damages Cry Trombone, and the cakes are ringed by popcorn, and the corn trinity manifests as: pancake the father, popcorn the sun, and the plate aura as the holy spirit. That's fine, I get it, I absolve you, but how do you respond to your late partner when he texts you:

Answer the question! Why did you not read and praise my work as soon as I sent it to you, though you were five hours away in Cambridge preparing for your presentation at Aardvark University?

You must have your priorities straightened by me and Being, *maintentant*: the work I assign you when you are in the midst of your own work and are most vulnerable: that is the thing you must first attend to. Because my envy is too much for me to throttle, it throttles me into present ancestry bar-chords of Fasterbeam Hauntages travel lore of bending toward Sawvein end of Oftober gossamer thinning of the blanket that separates the living us from the them that. That. That. But no! We're not so separa deadparate seepy sepsis pepsi sparta separate from the dead as we think. Here I just stepped over into that other world and--is anybody sitting here? You are now, take out your work and begin again with calm to sort through the papers of your birthcertificate all thirteen *boli* pain volumes of it and your transmigration certificate awaits swording, cut it in half

and bring it back together in different pieces with different doorways through to the backyard where you can chalk up the Belgrade courtyard wall with Tanya the violin player throughout your puberty summer and Mother will not let you go on a date with her to Tash Maydan Park because Mayday Mayday you are a pilot who breaks the sound burialmound layer Bangpop and you are not allowed to do that yet, you adolescent, come back into Mother and save her from loneliness by sewing yourself back into her womb with the brightest of redthread futuresutures Amen. Oh horryborry Amen. Recording session redbutton on. Not the nuke button. Recording in session. Quiet please. Silence is not existent. You can hear the dripping in the womb off-key and sliding back to the key of F flat manger: F is for Fasterbean Haunting the Vitriarch, the patriarchal virus haunted out of all of our bodies by Filip the pilot of

Fasterbean Damages airplane stuntwork flying through the groundbarrier deep into the earth's core to gather metamorphic and meta-Orphic rock and bathe in the magma of the Mohorovichich Discontinuity till it is renamed the Marinovich Bliss Spontaneity so the vanity of loneliness can dissipate as Fasterbean Damages turns back into his silkworm self in the core of the Earthbirthbigbangbongo Nebula. The bread you make in Francis Grove is fresh and safe for supplication. Thank you for remembering me to your grain silo. The missiles of the entire trackwork Earth have been relocated to Pluto where they we will freeze into the ice mountains. Here they are again. Mortar. Shells or what's there to put bricks together?

BETWEEN THE HEAVES OF STORM

Brenda told me to go to Zuccotti, that I wouldn't get arrested. Ariana said "I bet there are a lot of people falling in love here," looking over the sea of blue tarp tents. The Zuccotti Ocean wave washes away the dust of the greendollar crocus locust, and police state exuberance awakens from seeming Obama era hibernation to destroy us all for the health of the nation, a trickle down I.V. drip into the veins of only the rich and richest dust percent.

But these are obvious slobberings. Where was I going with this, Alicia? The draft rafts to the other side. Leave the raft behind, you can't carry it and get to the next place on the itinerary on the tour covering most of New England in red leaves and I had a feeling of mad hatter once. But I have to go back to Nude Whirlwind. Maybe we can go back to Australia five hours before we get there for the first time.

Waking up over the long cup, shuttle to Kneekirk. Husbands at kirke door I have had four: Oink, Oink, Oink, and Oinkbert. I had the idea of walking into a Zuccotti green tarp tent and emerging on the top of Akropolis, now hiring passionate baristas to service the democracy gods with nectar and ambrosia. Broth for the kids. The little kids. Baa! Baaaaah! Quiet down now, Johnson. It's just another failure Saturday, long in the rearview now. Execute. I killed an enormous fly

in my kitchen this morning when I died. The stillness in the air waslikemeflailingaroundwithadarkgreenbathrobeknocking the stuffed animal owl from the shelf to get at the fly. Finally I sprayed it on the high wall with the fruit and vegetable wash spray bottle. The fly fell on my spraying hand. I shook it off, sprayed it once more, and stomped it splat on the kitchen floor. Thus the death penalty has proven itself effective in my destroyed kitchen. The exonerated flies of the afterlife march forth wingless from the kitchen cupboard and strafe me with their dead wings flying from machine gun turrets in the plane belly bubble sky, the gibbous eye of an insect having vengeance on my deathdrive flesh, unbacked up since last night when I finally signed up for the cloud and synched and backed up my files so that my love and I can enjoy a long and happy afterlife in the backup files of the sky, vaporized by heat, light, and the solar flares giving us precognitive, or metacognitive eggnog experiences now, as we foretell the fly guests we will kill in our dreams, and wake up to pay for it with wrists bitten to the bone by actionfruit flies.

SHAKESPEARIAN MOTLEY COLLEGE

So I was thinking for the next class we could change things up a bit. I just get really jealous. We went on a happy hour crawl, all the parents in a coked out grotto--George W Bush's coke dealer went to Stanford--and we ended up at Zuccotti Park right in the middle of the occupation. Yeah, beer just adds unnecessary memories. The People's Library at Occupy Wall Street: many people say it is a friendly entrance portal into an intimidating place. But that's like double dating your mother and your aunt.

I have a high tolerance, I just like wet pavement, after a rainstorm, make love in a train, cross country, you infecting me in the sleeper car like I was Eva Marie Saint and you Cary Grant, the whole Mount Rushmore Mountain Range in your pants, top heads of state, such head, the kind of head you can only get in a train with the wheels and rocky motion collaborating through the sustained intensity fellowship granted by the Cassiopoiein constellation above, and only if you beg it for at least nine months.

"Don't be an artist, those are labor pains!" Uncle Dragon said on the banks of the Sava in Belgrade, but how did he know labor? He made his own printing company, Ars Grafika Beograd, but never gave birth to children, but did birth a lot of books into the world. The two species are not comparable, why they appear in the same sentence is to show how disguises fall off in close proximity to each other and we shower our skins off since we can't shed them with the same splendor as the serpents coiled around our ankles in the rutabagpipe garden, portending a future of dawn music, wakeup chords of the rooster throat in the year of the Chinese Fire Rooster Sky. I'd like to be there. I went to so many things I was never really there. Ew! Did it taste like booger? Did you go far? If you went to the drum circle and then the medicine tree of the shaman Michael during the fullmoon ritual you'll know the policewoman told us

"Turn the candles off, guys."

We blow out the mini wax votive candles.

LAURA WILL NOT BLOW OUT HER CANDLES
AT TONIGHT'S PERFORMANCE.

And so Michael produced a choir of battery powered votive flickering candle lights and we still had our light and dilated pupils to suck in the sky through tiny pinholes in our heads of conchshell beachbreak waveshells and wages. Moonstone pages of the dowry document shredded by King Lear when he cast his favorite daughter out for denying him a legal contract permitting incest. It's simply incorrect and

the whole family died to live it out and show us a map of how it may perchance to happen if we remain addicted to arrogance. If I bump into people then I was alive and allowed to bring ten more in. To Tenhell. I knew a friend there. Oh hay, he introduced himself. Good hay hath no peer, what ho, a bottle of hay, Father, better than any dowry thou couldst grant me. Daughters visiting. Lightning bolts, you're here for an hour, and we even less. The minutes sled down the hill and will not be counted.

Back in Zuccotti Park blue tarp tent, that's a good cover, it gets ripped off by strong October windgust

> *Ai ai ai ai*
> *Io io*
> *Io io*
> *Ai ai io io ai io io io*

Ionian island cove. Zakynthos Bay, stormracked, if you take a left past the Medicine Tent at Zuccotti. Temporal-Spaciode totes ripped open, would you like a cloaking device, well too bad, this is not the distant future past of your wet dream dossier scrolltongue stretching into outer space where you can lick the hanging out out of the lounge act and turn us all into a revolution which will again immediately devolve into bureaucracy. How to get it out of that cycle of knockwurst and cabbage and starving village of stumbling corpses. Two friends find it hard to part, our horses neigh as we wave goodbye to each other. God by you, Sir, whither? You just arrived and

you're supposed to have mental stability: like the first three months is all drugs. A palimpsest of hypocrisies and crises and Adderall gobbling tendencies make us friends by necessity under the same bluetarp stormtent. Oh Fool, I shall go mad. Oh Fool, I am so glad. There's one part of my vultureshredded heartbeak still sorry for thee. Art cold, my knave and puppy music stave? What sheetmusic flappeth in the dingey mothracket of soundwaves so au courant as to be illegible goblin prattle printed on the air by a three D printer? Why don't I be you and you be me? I'll forget my cellphone and you kiss me to return it. I do that all the time. Welcome to my routine eye. Let's pluck out the glass eyes of Gloucester and go bowling with them where the pins are toothpicks.

Smallville beckons! But it's not the usual miniature place. The twin vultures interview us at the gates and if we're not corpses we won't enter, so you better put on a good act. Simply look like you are walking through your most ordinary Wednesday

with a palm reading to look forward to later in the light of a Himalayan pink rose quartz salt lamp, for you cannot tell your future without it, you sold your intuiton at the yard sale with the Savory Island Summercamp tennis rackets.

                                                                                                       I don't care I still want to be a librarian where no one has to return any books and can bring the ones they want you to read so we can share the thundercommons speech, not screens, but screams evolving into voicings from where we don't know in our heads, hearths, and heaths, a heat language, a sun when you speak from the gut.

A SECTARY ASTRONOMICAL

With the Sun and Venus conjuncting this week I held a funeral for my desklamp at the sidewalk dumpster. Touching its beige shade I said: So long old friend, thank you for your service. No one talks to their lighting fixtures anymore. If I were a shipping crate would I carry a new gooseneck to you? Aren't I really carrion luggage looking for a couch to rest on? I'm keen to split my time between two analysts, a more and a less experienced one. My advisor will not let me, nevertheless, self-destruction unto extemporaneity be my perogative, talking wigrack that I am. Am I elm? I think I'm Norway Spruce, therefore I am. Remember when we were in the circle grove of pines and the ancient Russian man wandered in after us and said I THINK WE ARE PARTNERS WITH THE TREES ON THIS EARTH. Why are you enjoying it, memory, don't you have a life? Not at present, Dr. Javelin. But the substitute is excellent: I write to my friends, all of them, at the same time, it's known as correspondence at the core of time rock earth magma lava and the Marinovich Discontinuity, where liquid earth turns solid and vice versa in the other direction. Are you travelling toward the surface or the core? Yes.

"The Bush administration asked me to."

Whooo! That's not often something you hear at a coffeeshop in the West Village--or is it? There being no West or Village anymore. How cruel you are, Impermanence, and yet I don't want to call you Death. Not cruel but rather officious, strict, fell, the sergeant at the scene of arrest, a suicide note found pinned to my chest, the librarian comes running down the hallway to warn my my guidance counsellor I might kill myself. Do you think it a quirk of style I proceed in this way? But it will not come to me any other!

Do you prefer I change to make it utterly comprehensible to you, cave sibyl hanging upside down in the spelunker funk mansion ballroom, my acrobat reader, my blabbing semen, my lover, I mean you, cold pressed juice: carrot, orange, fingerlemon. A fingerlemon is peeled by severing your favorite finger from your hand and squeezing it into a juice glass and drinking it to see something new: it's hard to remain in one place and travel when you can't due to poverty and certain agoraphobias untreatable by the modern multispectrum medicines of the benumbers of state pharmacia. Then mail the fingerlemon to your lover. Even if your lover lives with you: send it through the mail. Your package has shipped! A moment of triumph. I could tell you about how much I love my comrades, how so much of the work of meeting remains sublimation. I don't want to talk with you much, I want to make love and then talk, don't you think it's much more honest, conversation, in that order? If you agree let's fuck to cut through the dead tape of our smalltalk. An occasional farm animal might wander by. There's one now, a cow, with a fourchambered stomach, just like we have a fourchambered heart to digest loves and die digesting and digesting them, digesting and digesting them as they digest us, as they digest us and die in us, and we are their coffins, a plus, a convenience for the global markets that don't need lovers like us getting in the way of consentual hallucination money. Why are you yelling? I'm not, we're discussing: to Americans passionate conversation between comrades foamrads often sounds like anger, white water rapids, but it's not, it's people not holding back with each other. What are you holding back? Would you like to tell me? You can yell at me if you want to, I'm used to it, having grown up in a Balkan family untrained in the art of passive aggression, expert in aggressive aggression, from which I withdraw to talk to you in a middle voice, a head voice when I start to sing falsetto wetdream seashanty of meeting you in secret so we can unpeel each other's fingerlemons and die simultaneously.

AT VESELKA

Last night I sit down at Baise bizou bizoucandy diner old Umra Ukranian Umla Umla Umlaut cloud. Last nicht I sit down. Last nap. Last nacht I nifty niftynighted de la nachtmusik in flight. Last night the flugelhorn stops halfway down my throwt.

Last night I sit down at Veselka diner and Dad turns to me and says "I have prostate cancer." No he didn't. He said

"Son, did you get my message?"

"No. I knew we were meeting for dinner."

"I have prostate cancer."

He said lamla la la la four day radiation treatment one hundred percent success rate, caught it early, lucky, etc

I could barely hear any of that THE BLOODPLUGS WERE IN MY EARS

Chicken paprikash on egg noodles please
I need protein right now so's not to pass out no pierogies.

Too bad it makes shitty poetry anyway. You would think:
A curse is also a gift: now I can write about it.
But no. It's just shit. And you can't flush it.
You have to sit with it.
Death death death death yours and everybody else's disappearance from the appletraum.

Do you appell me. What appellations may ai ai io io I fall
call you by that you will recognize me by.

Hi. My name is skinbag. Let us unpack itself
Not in preparedness
But on the go as we go
With all the Gods enlisted as helpers
All guardian guardiancestors notified as to the plight of
The wet freezing shivering raft mice.

One shivering mouse on the traction mat red before the
crosswalk over second avenue swiftflowing traffic river

Is that an aggressive thing to say James Joyce. Oh
Dear me these vibes in jeans
Have you felt the sun. Have you ever and won.
You can't win with a losing hand Bob Dylan sang
And the losing hand seems to be death
Hangman Hamlet Bang Sargent
Gambelot shat a dice pair onto the digits of
The driver on the speed course

Dad, I told you not to eat all that synthetic protein in the
energy bars and protein drinks before gym workouts
I told you they are known to cause prostate cancer
But no he went ahead and kept gobbling and drinking
And now the spray barista comes around with
Blue detergent spray bottle to hustle us out
Even though the coffeeshop has not closed yet
These people want to go home
How short is life
Shorter than this coffeeshop stay
Todaynight todayfornight

Todaynightfornight fort for please do not
Spray your blue detergent juice in my face
I just barely slipped free of the noose and now
It's time to go already
I don't drink or smoke weekends anymore
But I eat latenight applesauce jar and watch
Spotlight movie to see how I can be a journalist
And root out the psychopathic pedophiles in my own
Head before they happen.
It all already happened. Hap. It's not a happy end.
Thoughts like fat rinds of deathlemons
Drop to the floor
Who's peeling them?
I need to go back to my Dad's apartment
And rescue Stanzas in Meditation by Gertrude Stein
Before the mold gets to it from the flood
That broke through the apartment heat pipes
At New Year, a New Year's Present from Father Time,
Kronos, Saturn, always readying us for the urn
By burning pieces of us to ash cinders gnats mice lizards
Regeneration and death in the one-two-two step
Always dance and that's a great theory
But right now I can't feel it I feel a throb pain in my ribs
Knocked out of me is the wind
Is the wind here
Can the wind come to the phone please
And help me up out of this hunchback position I slouch in
As if the growing hump on my back is a lantern
That will grow its flame to light my way
It won't it won't only I can do that
And I have help from friends too
Though where they are now is dealing with their
Own deaths too.

COYOTE BANANAS

How was your January? Hellish, how was yours? I went to Australia before the storm. Wow. How long is the flight there? Epic. Did you watch movies? Not a lot. My thoughts don't stress me out much. Are you a meditator? No. Whoa. You are a meditator. Service dog knows. He goes: wark wark wah wark wah wah wah wah warkward. Better than awkward. Is that cup working for you? The lid won't fit. LOOKING FOR PASSIONATE BARISTAS. Fasterbean Damages is hiring. Experience is a necessity. Here, have a new cup. The old cups were discontinued, for they were defective. Now the lid fits. Our hands touch as you pass the cup to me and take away the old one and place the red heat shield band around the new cup in my hand the white and red and blue and gold cup in my hand hot. Do you want milk in it? Please, yes. You have a good one. No, you.

No you no me no ears no nature of our predecessors no eyes no nose no tongue tuberose. No obstacles because no mind to be beobstacled. And yet. The fete. What is there to celebrate now. Our consciousness. As it leaves the Aeon with the Aeon. The Aeon cannon fires to help the rebel ships escape past the imperial blockade. Darth Vader has no good little man inside him. The little old weak man does not pull levers behind the green Wizard of Oz curtain. No one's there. Controlling things. Maybe a shadow government or two. Or is that wish fulfillment, a desperate attempt to imagine someone behind the scenes controlling things? Two to midnight, atomic scientists move the clock, two minutes until nucelar ecocidal larvageddon armament blow up polar ice cap sink the world into the outer space from whence it came. We know! We know!

But what to do in those last 120 seconds. This strawberry is delicious! This strawman tastes like my dad when I used to kiss him mornings before he shaved and I called him Cactus Face and he said don't call me that and I was just a kid but already loved naming things because I was not free to do things I wanted to do. Father will prevent you. But not anymore. Dad told me in the middle of January Janus month of twofaced coinhead sparkly bait liar and deceiver extraordinaire. Just before we order dinner at Veselka Diner

Dad utters the Dadspeech death butterstick tongue wagging pronouncement shock: *I have prostate cancer, he says.*

For the next two weeks I live underwater, watching movies with him, eating dinners with him, listening to him bark back at me for no reason, slowly losing his calm mapper mind. The slide into nutmeg grinderdom. Brown powder we come out the other side to spice the food of future foodture vulture hen generations without knowing it. Senseless. Endless. Nen. Nowheart, come back. After two weeks Dad texts me:

Fil the Thrill, it's inflamed prostate, not cancer, on antibiotics for four weeks, am fine. Misdiagnosis.

Relief! I read it and then take off into the Eclipsenight Scissors snip snip light freeing me from the marionette Marinovichstringsofanxietymomentarily. Dad--DESTROYED. Dad--NOT DESTROYED. Then NEN NEN I had the Dad dream and still the Aeonending fire will come but AEONENDING contains NEN in it, and we can prevent nuclear holocaust with togetherness nen, nowheart, not corporatocracized mindfullness for meditative pushing of nuclear buttons, whose is bigger, the red button clit envy of psychotic male dictator patriarchy. Then I had the Dad dream:

Woman friend hands me Hallucinogen white gum rectangle slab
I eat it

>   (How are your white bloodcells?
>   I interrupt to text Mom)

It's too much—the hallucinogen at the party--why did I take it? I thought it would let me see the situationscissors more clearly snip snip cutting all threads to my previous consciousness and ideas of progress—

Dad--help! I ask my dad the chemist to help me get out of this bad hallucinogen trance. What Dad says to do doesn't help now with this fire in my mouth—speechgum skullucinogen--HALLUCINOGANSETT, LONG ISLAND—

So I talk to the great friendwitch luminous personage helping me to digest my poisonous actionfruit karmaphalam Valhalla pear tart gluttony—I ask her what to do--I say CHARCOAL TABLETS! Yes, she agrees—

I fly through the window from the second story party in a red gondola ski lift car—slam on the street—get out—go to bodega—

Bananas will help--but they
                      only have

                COYOTE BANANAS!

Spiny bumpy smaller bananas with tufts of brown coyote fur around their middles when you unpeel them--

Tricksterbananas! You can't trick them—

I get them but know I won't eat them—

I stare at the unpeeled coyote bananas on the bodega display stand inside the store. The reddish brown tufts of coyote fur around the banana midriffs warn of possible digestion obstacles but also promise great antidote powers to me who took too much white gum rectangular hallucinogen at the party.

Two days ago I was reading Emily Wilson's limpid new translation of Homer's Odyssey, the Circe Episode, on Circe's island of Aeaea Aeonic Fire Aeaea Island. The patriarchy is revealed in its true nature: pigs! Circe never changed them to pigs, she merely revealed to them what they already are, in their war gear for permanent war dressed they were. Oink oink slaughter. Circe gave them the hallucinogen herbs for them know self. Odysseus escaped this fate by getting an antidote from Hermes: Moly root,
Milky yum shake from the ground, only Gods know how to pull it out.

When I consulted my father in the dream as to what to about my bad hallucinogen sickness I turned into the pig paralysis, because he is the Patriarchy. When I consulted the woman friend and relied on my own wisdom, I remembered the antidote charcoal and found the coyote bananas and saved myself with my own imagination from pigdom patriarchal slaughterhouse. Or did I? By listening to father patriarchy you are a pig,

However, when you investigate for yourself
What this age is
You live
   eyes
LIVE YES
LIVE EYES

Father Destroyed Father Not Destroyed

What difference? Spend time with your father before he dies whether he's dying or not he dies and you die and mother dies and there is no mother or father or you or anybody now when now when now is a time when NEN NEN now come back now to Nowheartmind. Oink. Begin.

Hang off the cliff of the Aeonending fire wave flame crest and pluck the fruit, peel, and eat it

This coyote banana is delicious!

Yelp yelp whelp whelp yelp woof wark warkward woof warp, the coyotes call inside me now in bananakalpafragments.

LAVENDER BENDER FOR JOANNE KYGER
to Julien Poirier

We're so lucky she
visited. This is too much loss of
elders.
Way too much.
Now it's us.
Is it too late to grow up?
WAY TOO LATE

I type with my thumbs after sucking on them
Oral fixation not oral tradition
Or
        Seehorse smells so good.
        Seehorse has lavender blood.
        Rabbit is a coconaut.
        Why?
        Because Rabbit explores space
        in the coconut milk sky
visited. This is too much loss—

Elders—
rest in woodshed.

I shed the fear of
madness (in jest
madness (clinical
        (artistic
            madness you fake when
    you want to be alone
to get some work done.

        Pal, buddy, pallbearer,
she died yesterday at eleven.

All of us are living outside
what we're actually living in.

Grief antler hat
always comes back
for you to wear it
again but
your grief is changed.

      Seehorse smells so good.
      Seehorse has lavender blood.
      Rabbit is a coconaut.
      Why
      Because Rabbit explores space
      in the coconut milk sky
visited. I'm so
elder
I'm going into the woods
for a bath
Rabbit
this grief hurts so hard I need a target to sparrow toward

ANYTHING
TO GET THESE GRIEF HANDS OFF ME
GROPING ME AS IF I WERE HOT

      I'M UGLY
      GRIEF
      GET A CLUE

AND WITH THAT
GRIEF LEFT ME ALONE
IN MY WALKING SHOES
IN MY MOUSE GLUETRAP SANDALS

to disappear into the ramble
hot to cruise
to listen to bluejays bully each other into fantastic blue flash
bushes
not death
        the courages return
as courage worms
poking through the red wet soil
of my forehead as my fever breaks
         so I can walk again I can talk
    with Joanne.

Why should a ringworm president live
and you have no breath at all?
But your breath is in me now
for walking,
waking —
    "wakka wakka wakka" —
as the purple Pac Man ghosts once sang
at the video arcade in Riverdale New York the Bronx the
U.S. the world the chiliocosm the multiverse poof planets
poof poof planets puff puff pass planets pass —

        smoke or
fumes or mist or breath or applesauce earphones get into the
middle ear where you can really hear the apple tree growing
up through your neighborhood concrete sidewalk —

        w h o
planted it nobody did and you are still my best friend you
you who I you with as I you myself out of here into Central
Park entrails to bow to the red-tailed hawk who killed a
pigeon in the snow last winter and perched on top of it to
show it was his.

Dear red tailed hawk,
depression becomes a refuge to do no harm in—
help me out of this
package damaged in transport.

I always forget how psychedelic grief is.

Caffeine does help it speed away doesn't it
And you find yourself under the unlocked tray table
In an airplane—how did you get this way—
And what is the destination?
The debriefer wouldn't say
Before he took your skin off and hung it on a coat
hanger.

It feels shameful to walk in sunlight since you are dead
Joanne and I am too bad a poet to write you the appropriate
requiem but then my specialty never was the appropriate
but driving ninety miles per hour into a redbrick dead end
full of drill bits I swallowed as meds,

                                        commuting to
work over the George Washington Bridge because it is a
brontosaurus skeleton

and we have successfully outbrontosaurus'd ourselves,
outsourced breathing to the exoplanets

sending us signals from Radiowave Park
where THE SHADOW still echoes its episodes
THE SHADOW KNOWS where we're going
it's already there
with Ikkyu in the fish market jaguar house.

I cry so much my tears will delouse me
burn down my body all night long
as the heater clanks its percussion-only song:

> Package damaged in transport
> Is anything missing yet
> I always forget
> SURGERY FOR MY CAT MERLIN.

Thank you Joanne for leaving out the love sign astrology book
for me to find
and forget for a moment
Truman lies extend
into nowtime orange wigrack skeleton--

I see Trump at the intermission of a Neil Young solo show at Carnegie Hall:
He's chatting with Charlie Rose in the front row.
Trump and Rose both team players for the United States entertainment complex of American exceptionalism
Exceptionally stupid, dangerous, and ecocidal.

Ranting
R train
My nervous system's a rake
And I'm the orange leaves under it

Speeding away from Seehorse
As if I could find her in the Ramble trees
Forestbathing one hundred city blocks away from me.

I wish I had a scalpel that could cut off the Wall Street
Tip of Manhattan
Where she works
Then she could never work there again
And she would become known and justly celebrated as
The great writer she already secretly is.

Outside the Ramble
On the hill of the Doggoze
The big old greying golden retriever enthroned
Growls but
Learn from him how to sit
Not caring about the cold
Back to the sun.

New York's a prison
At Trump Rink
Central Park
Do the skaters know
Whose structure they skate on?
Yes they skate to throw the structure away.
It will not work but neither will this constant
Judgment perception you precipitate—
Thunder snow in your skull does not make you great,
American owning a gun,
And discharging it for freedom
Into the sky, that rash intruder on your property—

AUTHORIZED
VEHICLES
ONLY

NO GREATER OR LESSER VEHICLES ALLOWED
BEYOND THIS POINT
FROM EIGHT O' CLOCK TO SIX O' CLOCK PM
                      I am
                beyond red
          Japanese maple leaf
     sad about Joanne.
Fucking A they're all dying.
Berkson Meltzer Kyger.
What do we do?
Go to pharmacy
Find burial mound.

       O when will we all have all the love we need
       Never or next Christmas Eve
       Always I thank Adam and Steve
       Genesis Genes made me a magical being

            For a proper sketch of my present anatomy
            Please turn the page
            To Rippety Rabbit
            Curer of the plague of sadness
            With sanity laughter
            I'm all alather
            Alather
            Alather
            Alather

DOGEN'S TWO THROWNNESSES

A. I will go forth and experience the myriad things = Delusion.

        (The light is not penetrating freely.)

B. The myriad things experience themselves = Wakeup.

        (I cling to Wakeup and again
        the light does not penetrate freely.)

Perhaps the real delusion is that there is a linear development between A and B.

B and A weave in a sideways 8 pattern of silk time.
That gets cut
At some point, we don't know when,
Though other threads go on.
Red threads are among them!
The time of the red thread returns!

Red thread fever burns. Nevertheless, on!

I think writing can be a time when we can let go of A and be as B as possible.
In a B type of writing
the words experience themselves,
the syllables experience themselves,
the rhythms experience themselves,
the voices around you are not separate from the voices within you,
nor is there "in and out" anymore,
but rather timespace manifesting itself as present voices written on a page or screen, (or voiced in air as air as thin air dictionaries of preliterary languagings, as the

mountains in the mountains, singing, deliver the full moon baby, We Me Wheeling A/B Sansui Sandsea,) the voices experiencing themselves as letters as timebeing as mystery that cannot be said or written:

the closer I get here the farther away I remain, remains, R.E.M.,
Rapid Eye Movement Diocese,
Vapour, with a British spelling, for more island mist in it through the "u"
You I E O A and always Y
The Vowel Joy,
   i i

I love your hat! Thanks, it's a bucket hat. Have you ever written a song called Bucket Hat? No. I was telling somebody earlier, but they weren't listening, that Gazpacho would be a good name for a song. Do you know what Gazpacho is? Yes! gaz gaz gaz gaz gaz and a tower of coffee lids toppled by the wind coming in through the door now opened at the coffee shop closing at 6:30pm so that everybody doesn't stay up all night there and kill themselves with an overdose of caffeine and, when the tolerance to it is built up, the switch to crystal methedrine so popular in the Sudafed States of Pharmaticon Artistry.

But what does this have to do with Yunmen's Two Sicknesses? Well, we've outgrown them, we have "MEDS" now, little candies for kids and adults as well. "MEDS" keep us well, well enough, near the town well where the girl is stuck and crying out and the firemen cannot save her in time, and this is a news item and then forgotten. How do you make the news that stays bluesy enough to ring out true even long after it's due for the printer, and the papers are tossed in the garbage, or the news is lost in the internet filedump? The present is a magnet that attracts words that last to it if you can concentrate with ease, Samadhi and Sandra Dee on the same seesaw laughing

    clank clank clank plank gangplank Mayflowering

Sincerely,
Filedump Marinovich Spermbank Whale Sea
Reporting live
With the kids here again
"BOOKS NOT BULLETS"
"BOOKS NOT GUNS"
Meds are bullets
Dissolvable in gullets
That can make kids kill
Or possibly stop them
Or make them kill again
With the second amendment
Hunter machine guns
For the deer we are
And the venison we will be
American Eating

    Landfill Dictionary

HAMLET LE PENDU

Are you hanging upside down yet. I don't know you. Are you the hanging man or Odin Overdose. Too easy. You don't know me yet and never will you. I am Reagan Reaganatomy Reagnomics Reaganstarwars Gentle Regan O Reagan not the need Reason Reason teach me treason if it means defecting from these untitled states so be it.

I defected to Russia and became the American Baryshnikov ballet rockstar with smuggled Kalashnyikov legs I dance on point and fire at the proscenium surface to show the state at work as a choreography practice. The reptillians among us clap with our green webbed hands. What can we catch with them. Flies for nourishment.

Where there are humans you will find fois gras, flies, and Buddhas, yes, Issa, but who has the strength to stick the baster down the goose throat and fill the bird full of fat and good red wine until its liver explodes and since when is a goose an it. This is an animal rights ad. This is the Seventh Anomaly from the Sun, the asteroid Chiron, the wounded healer socalled because he will wound you, and heal yourself then. You will get no help from him until you teach your own specific secret humiliating wound:

I gave roofies to mine Uncle Claudius and now I make love with him on my Mommy's mattress where I tied her up in bandages so she could watch from a front row seat for damages. How is my anal lining doing Mommy. Are the mucous membranes intact. Has the Aids entered yet. Have Reagan's aides been to the scene and back bringing necessary government aid to the sick the wounded the castrated elephants with ivory tusks stuck in the Capitol dome to make DC known. Known as what Cornhusk whispering when the wind hits it just right you can hear its hustler wheeze as the cornmaze invites you in for a night of hanging by your feet from the oak tree at the center of it named Shameboot because you will fall out of your shameboots by the end of the night and walk with bare feet over the glass broken in your own teeth while you drink the red wine from it. I don't drink wine from anything but my lover's hiking boots anymore. Shameboot medicine. Where's my prescription. I forgot it at the sliding doors to the Torn Bandage. Gag me. Gag me with your balled up bandage, Mommy. Let Polonius watch us through the curtain hole where I stabbed him dead. The curtain is red and so is his blood and it's red on red painting I love on red lodge wallpaper above the sun when I get going and the asteroid belt slips from my waist I'm loose in this place deep outer space where big daddy Jupiter the gas giant fucks me asleep with his gigantic swirling orange ballgag gagging me so I can fly further and further on into the next galaxy where I know no more names of planets and have to live with die with the nameless nameless nameless namelessnesses yes

MANIC MIXTURE 7 FAILURES IN THE FISH

Respond to
How are you
With
Hey how's it going
That way nobody ever says
What nobody's feeling

....
COMMENTARY :

Is Molly your height? No but I don't feel like we're that far off. I can't buy any piece of alternative specifics. It has to be beast parts to ingest so I can get beastie on my encumberances of chrome in the fiddle distance. Let's say that you're eating the same thing: so you're having twelve bowls of cereal around your bed. You're not crazy, you came without a truck, you know what will happen to you if you don't the dagger duck. Dog year is about entertainment: there goes a fox dog now, begging for food from his master. Alright, where's Hollywood? Like a similar architecture see what you are evading. This coffee is about a journey--a journey to entryway to roasty pepper gateway to gay coffee experiences beyond the coffin spaceship you behold beyond the bezonder yawn of Merryman the Merperson. Merpersons of interest. Caravan Lisp and the biting children. It occurs to me I'm still a faggot no matter how much marriage armor I wear. I will confuse people and myself in the process but I love her and her serene in-the-gymnasium-all-day poker face and will not be dissuaded from loving her in our purple bed even if we sleep in shifts. Insomnia. Grief. Shared grief is not love yet but it's a good beginning. We have nothing.

Just stay in my apartment now. What are we signalling? SOS to the aliens? They won't save us. They're us and we don't want to be saved just to have a good time on the way down. I wish it was Wednesday then I would be here to eat you. Today I'm golden flakes glinting against the aquarium bubble light goldfish food. Orange mood. High alert attitude. I really enjoyed last night getting shit done, sculpturally we have no inhibitions but applied salary. It's okay to hold that bag of fat green funk buds on the restaurant table, thank you, we're in California, thank you addiction and function malfunction cycles to organize the time obliteration.

Be careful on the stairs. Be especially careful when carrying a load. Be risky on the stars. Be especially risky when downloading a scar.

When you come I'll take you to the wedding. Hopefully I'll have a new job. The millenial ways of not responding to a friendship text are dendrite mysterious and various: surely I will not pretend to know anything. I will dwell in the house of the myriad forever. You are evicted. Foreclosed. What do you do now. Dose. Doze. Mow the lawn. Wait for my foreskin gown to regrow itself down my chess pawn. Where do we sit down where we're not littering. Where all that glitters gold is not listening, surveillance twistering.

I'm like this little wolfman who walks around putting icecubes in my wine. This wolfman comes running up and he's like I'm crazy, I saw you're mom last week. And then there's like my mom, living and dying and timing, how is the timing behind it? Never perfect never decent perfectly naked and offkey recent. Waiting in the bathroom line at the yogurt place is the new cause celebre of the long line. Like, Sonoma's down here, I had never worked a wine show before but now can sample many flavors before I fall against the dungeon door.

You're struck with me for a while.
I will do my best to obey you, Mistress.
Do you remember Freddy Elixir? No
I don't understand what he's saying. What's hap-
Pening now to any one ship—
Is this where the water's coming out?
Titanic gout
In ship feet
Ouch
Iceberg couch
Like a year and a half between Bedford and First Avenue
If the person becomes unresponsive
Continue rescue breaths and

The coffee's getting cold. Order another one to not go. To stray and snow inside like a cloud that got lost in the coffeeshop cum yogurtshop. Probiotic havoc of guts stripped of essential populations in the biome gone hiking.

Now do you have cups for water
Matter
Mater
Milk
Triple capp
Skinbag map
Timeline vamp?
No.

Try onion rings of the Inferno. Are you hungry or? No. I need another coffee before I snow on the valley below. As a storm front marriage is never easy.
There is no back door
Where I belong in candor.

It's after grace. Seven after. What clock are you using? Velocoraptor. Velocity rapier Hamlet bodkin dock. What's o' clock, thou knave? Grapes in the Hades terrain arid and foggy for the Pinot-holic within thee, prolix prince, dense markmaker of glossolalia spelled out on the wide ruled lines of forehead pages. How many heads did you have to take to make that scroll? None but my own or mine own depending on the time I'm droned by democracy's snow.

HOCKNEY WATER

Come on David admit it. Shower in a tall red teabox with crustaceans. Listen to two old ladies laugh at the male on male 69 position. Cos two men together are naturally comical. What would you prefer war.

Yeah. It's illusion. They rediscovered that in the Rennaissance when I was born through a silver mesh reflected in the reflexes of school crushes appearing next to phallus-like forms, allowing me to ignore the conchshell of illusionistic space and paint merrily in a flat style. With the chorus of hacking coughs far behind me now, I ambled into the next gallery at West Yorkshire to take a shower in a tall black flower pot. The red rotary phone hung from sheet music lines in the corner, beige as when it rings and wakes you and you go to the door to receive a package with your mouth. The kindness of mailmen abounds.

Rolled up unprimed canvas is a scroll to hit your head with. It's percussion breath tempo we're after in this rehearsal meadow. Get away from me, med vendor. I can't speed with you inside me. Can't tambourine. Wink back at me, tiny red pink white apron shrunk in the washing machine. Woman in back of me brushes against my back with her breasts for a thrill for the both of us, unacknowledged, flirtier that way. Chilly like a meatball.

People truly know how to move through chlorinated timespace right now. It's almost like they're breaking the intimate fourth wall. Like, I know there's so many portraits of people looking out at us, flirtatious, doing blow with Johnny Depp, so much love, powerstruggling. The profundity floors me. I am down there, a green gumstain.

And then the guy is judging me, just because I swim in tighty-whities. Dude, mind the commentary. I can't tell if it's pink or blue or wealthier—where is he from? London. Are the majority of his subjects from London? Are you a white guy? Oh, you're good. Puke. Is he still alive?

People panic, voicing their opinions today, as if the paintings would disappear the minute we stop talking them down from the precipice over our unacknowledged desires. How dare the nudes reveal to us what we want from flesh. How dare you do this to us in your tighty whities, pool boy, making your last underwater lap, holding your breath, training for virtuoso fellatio. No flash. No recording please no recording thank you.

MERCREDI SKIIS

Loup Maison. Grey wing above a green roof. Wood. Wood. Woof! Construction: it eliminated a lot of shelves. Starry floor of inconvenience. Oil and ink on linen. You cannot repeat it here or release it elsewhere for show, for now the auditors expect you and cannot be ambushed. Ambient sounds drift in and it is not a contest. Open your bison. If I have a maison haibun head I get rid of the pain of being human. That's why I left. I got wired from looking. The glass looked back at me and the drawing drew me till I was out of crayons. Umbilical kitestring attached at the coffin. Red Walton. Pirate from the engraving. Where is the crayon sharpener in this prison. No I won't step out of the way for you to take your phone picture. Unless you ask me: we are human beings. Don't exaggerate. We are phones with attached bodies drifting between soda machines: birth and death and the taxes are an aphrodisiac in spring. It makes me steady. Springes to catch woodcocks as Shakespeare said. I shook for him to become a fashionable narcoleptic in a red barn crashing on an Iowa road I've never been on. Lame Maison, I limp back and forth before the pink house to screw my courage up to ring the front doorbell. The marauders left a dead bird on my doorstep. This was not a sign but I took it for one and became a spy for no one. I report to bleeding gums and the kissing airport technicians on the runway not seeing the plane about to take off their heads. Acephalic dread. I would invite you over but you're my friend and you appear when I open the door least expected: the desk drawer in the forehead where I keep my wedding ring, a piece of red Cecilia yarn in its circumference, and a pack of Marsielle tarot cards. If you come too close to the painting the alarm goes off. You can hotwire a painting and drive out with it. The mausoleum is closed now. Please make your way to the nearest exit wound: the one with the John F Kennedy brains on the lapels of the resting people before Trump Tower now taking pictures of its seven pointed black glass tops as if the camera would suck up the power and give them some. But I am superior I don't give into such distraction. Excuse me a car just hit me. It was hitting on me and then it got some.

THE HALIBUT ARMS

Sunface mood now Moonface mood now
Don't call it a disorder
Disrobe and we'll order in
And fuck three times before the food gets here
Only to be interrupted by a quick noodles
Followed by one more cock slurpdown
Encore encore
Dolce far niente
The dulcet sounds of doing nothing far away
The construction site beneath our purple queen bangs away at the weak nonresidential edifice of sleep

but it won't happen because I'll be alone bingewatching "Love" and I'll dip a banana into the no-fat yogurt and suck the cream off the tip like it's you and no one will tell any one any of it and we will go on sublimating it until there's no it but the it that hits you inside your head and knocks you out of your movie watching chair and you pull the blue bathrobe over you and bury yourself

                                                you can say a final word before you are interred in the earth in the floor of your apartment to await rebirth at the hands of the cockatoo man who just closed his exhibit and travels on to show his white blue green feathers to other muses who will encourage him out of his box while you are busy breeding phlox

Include the fact of your being married
Include the obstacles to the desire
Along with the desire
Equally
And the difficulty in
Defenestrating crushes

O Defenestrado
How do you survive the fall from a hundred glassy bluegreen UN stories

It's a frozen lake you lie on while the dead crusty sunflower silhouettes grow out of your thighs let's take you to bed and eat sushi are you hungry yet you're not really dead you're just playing a sex game where I take you for being limp and harden inside you

I like it when you throw my thighs up around my neck
And push yourself down on me
Crush me into the bed
Heck that's we three in the purple sheets
Ouroubros can't touch it we are clambake amplifiers blasting music from a live Billy Joel cover band flown in for the fata morgana bourbon mixer at summer camp the handjobs were great but then I had to fly away to Yugoslavia to see my grandparents I remember warm water running off my feet in the community shower down the silver drain that did glisten and then I didn't sprain my ankle I rained from my cloud cockatoo face

I like it when you enter me and it hurts and I say ouch

I like it when I'm on top of you and you stick your ringfinger in my ass because we are married but don't wear our rings anymore
At the check-in desk to the Hotel Halibut Arms
The halibut arms himself against mercury in the water he absorbs through his gills

That's Gillian with a hard G like gills

You'd think it was a soft G
But I like it when you touch my G-spot
With your cock when I'm on top of it and can control nothing

I got off
I didn't come on your belly though later you said I could have

Cum on the belly would be wonderful
And write to me about how
It feels when I'm inside you
Do you like it all the way to the basement
Or teasing the rim

Fill me up we'll talk later when I'm wounded for now I want it rough or you rough and me pinned with my knees at my ears and you jackhammer away until I can hear the scream and not know it's me it's coming from both of us through shattered skylight skin we bleed each other uninfected kissing with our whole bodies no yield no stop sign no traffic island just this highway male on male flesh pounding surf drone tubular and negative blood pool clotting above our heads the ceiling is populated with tiny white dot dwarves watching over us disinfecting our blood with the tears they cry on us

SLEEPING THROUGH THE DAYS AND COMMUNICATING WITH EMIGRE FRIENDS

I was at a summer resort possibly in Georgia, America—background brought in from bingewatching by the brain—and my friend Julien and I and other friends were all shooting heroin into our feet for this one summer we decided we would kill pain this way. No pain no pain no pain, as trainer and fighter said in ROCKY IV, an instructional masterpiece of Cold War propaganda. Shoot dope in the webbing right between the toes. And then I was hooked but then I said no on the traffic island no more. And my friends Julien, Mike, and Anteater Esophagus Turnpike said

Nooooo do not leave us lonely without a fellow spike.

And I said goodbye. But there I was at Jeffrey Joe's gas station shack kicking and depressed and summery in a short blue dress and Jeffrey Joe promised to take me in the back and talk me up to the sky so I could be reconciled with it. To live not die.

To live, Mother! hills! Georgia! basalt ganglia! ganglion furze

frozen wounds between toes. Jeffrey Joe Julien porridge in a bucket hat.

ARE YOU GOING FISHING ON NEW YEAR'S DAY FILIP AND CAN YOU TELL ME THE TEMPORAL COORDINATES THAT I MAY JOIN YOU a fellow fisherman at the gas station asks but

I DON'T KNOW I'M GOING BEHIND NOW THE GAS SHACK TO LISTEN TO THE COACH JEFFREY JOE PEP TALK AND THEN WE'RE GOING TO THE NORTH CAROLINA TREEHOUSE FOR DETOX.

Where is it? 20 minutes.
Morgan, how are your secrets today?
Ah—one too few.
You? Still steady and golden
Great secret factory
Every breath yeah
Vertical uh
        earth--

Oh I looked up the band Flirty Scree.
The feminine energy on the planet is very strong now
After being repressed for so long.
A reorganization. Can we put the chairs in a circle
Cos I have a hard time concentrating otherwise?
When I worked as a barista I did it one to one
A coarse grind. No we cannot change the arrangement of
The seats. We just did. The power struggle continues. Then
You buy a bottle of affect. I moved from Bed Stuy
To the Parkside Q. The first time I became really good
Friends with my roommate.

Do I seem angry? That's cos I am. Not really. I took a Pan-Am flight here today from my homeland of Yugoslavia and now will address you in the second person as the universal you you know yourself to be. And how about that apartment we last saw each other in, you don't like to breathe much through the key hole do you unless you are peeping through and through and through it.

You forgot to set the timer for twenty minutes.

La la la, Sunday rehearsal dinner, who gets married this early in the week to his own late wife, bringing her back from the termites, we were two coffee tables that got married and she was taken first by the termites and I will not follow far behind.

How come in the picture of the red room inside the supposedly same red room there is no one on the red couch but now two friends sit on it? Terrence and Sarah, hello! Without you I would be lead in water pipes poisoning the whole family as it sipped English beak pterodactyl tea breakfast liquid television IV drip from the flat screen sentences running across the wall, a green stock market crawl of digits fleeing the insecticide spray of parents and policemen alike.

I'm going out to get juice does anybody need anything?

Smelling salts and soda and acorns for the squirrel in me to free itself from ribcage quarantine.

I can't make out the lyrics next door but the ukulele sounds as out of tune as my front door this morning when I made my way to you, a rusty sparrow

I want a gavel and I want a long wooden table and that's where my depressions are made and can be thrown out the window with the long red curtains and plastic sheets of the winterized brownstone Chelsea palace, but as an actor too you're not on stage in the movies, you're not feeling that energy of reception, and if they have chips you don't really eat them they're just garbage, you're out all day watching snow fall on hay, the stormfront moves over the farm you've never been to,
Welcome to the uncomfortable foaming desert oasis,
I'm on the board.

Did everybody do something nice yesterday did everybody stay in
The year two thousand
You should get the coconut icecream and hide it
You need to make a sculpture and put all your icecream in it
Avocado charcoal
Neural deficit of the year
I didn't feel like being alone but I felt like a loner
Does that make sense I think a piece of hail just hit me on the nose
As if the present were some translation machine between the past and the future
Where is it
It's so weird that a hardware store would have suitcase trees
It's toxic to look for reasons not to do things
Am I on the best wait list possible
I think it's important that you always live before
Because if you wait to live
You'll never live.

SYNOPSIS CYCLOPS

Filip Marinovich stars as a Serbian emigre in Manhattan who believes that, because of an ancient curse, any physical intimacy with the man he loves (Kent Smith) will turn him into a feline predator.

If that really happened I would find a way to contact you and plus I have this thing where I'm a part time psychic

>and my feet churching steps
>>earn a cool night like Shalimar
>>>history book shoe plants.

When I teach I feel like each one of us has the mild form of brain damage called living online. Each of us is afflicted with illiteracy in our own way: the owls fly from our shoulders and the collarbones tear themselves free of our skins and skeletal systems and the coffeeshop neighbor points his dirty sneaker at my thigh. Can we squish in? I'm the worst at COMING INTO MANHATTAN for the weekend away from home along the Cabot cheddar fault with the mice biting for earthquake. Demean 'em. Who? The mice! They are all your tourmaline relatives reincarnated under the earth's crust to continue your torment: an educational must.

>I walked away, I was just being too mean to me.

Tried for treason I visited the Container Store
Under the supervision of two police Centaurs.

Finally the two of you leave, I take over your seats and bleed internally until each app I download opens simultaneously on each phone screen in the imbalance infirmary of misfiring chemicals to say: I love your rings by the way. It's crazy. I thought I lost the stone. Still reign. Stillborn frame. I think tears like flew like projectile. Thank you I love origins. In Centaur culture it's traditional to wear red. I work with caterers all night. Within two weeks I was like I want to kill myself. I was not on video but I wanted to hide. Giddy with life. A Gideon's Bible in each of my hotel cupboard drawer eyes.

WHY I AM NOT STRAIGHT

I throw the trash out first thing Tax Tuesday morning and there's already a Gay Pride Rainbow flag in the garbage WHY does life have to be so symbolic and sassy and slap me first thing this afternoon as I emerge from nocturnal combat lair insomnia chamber unenclosed sidewalk cafe? Where is the ex and where the interior of encroaching dementia in my infinitely marketable gerontophile rom-com sodomite life? I confide in my director: I made a work friend. Okay, but did you do any work?

No friend, no work, as we like to say this deep in the gingerbread oven where we rise, little boys and girls with witches and witch doctors of the workplace of paid slave labor where the abusive hollering administrative assistant is never fired because "That's just Drama being Drama." Not helpful! I have a three minute persona that just expired. Are you aware of anything developing behind me now, is my own funeral pyre coming on to me? Stop hitting on me, you oiled logs and flames. Thou kindling on a Troy beach. Whatever, that's not me. I'm here for a large Corsica, beloved blend with dark chocolate notes that whack you on the rear end and get you breathing when you assume the stillbirth position just outside the day's womb. Wake up and let you be you be you be you. Benumb you. No. The ice on my right booster rocket O-rings stinks of future fuel leakage and will show engineers the threat to my fuselage before I lift off, or my name isn't the Challenger Ronald Reagan AIDS Denier Reentry Columbia. The dove of war swoops down and claims my eyeballs with its beak in two swift moves. Hi! How are you? Good luck to you and our remaining contestants. Treasured Severance, measure the end of air, its resumption, and the various incoming clients voicing their concerns on

how to take spleen by force and never feel it again. I had to work early this morning so I could get to my shrink on time. I like my new shrink. He is an inkwell and talks marriage with the best of them: Bloodsport Venice he calls it, as if it's honeymoon all the time, and we just have to show up to the airport interrogation chamber with our tickets for the plane that will not take us away because something strange has been found in our bloodwork:

we are all immigrants from the big bang, grounded, infantilized on tarmac, getting our fingerprints taken by fellow skinbags with non-toxic foam inkpads for the health of our freshly incarcerated fingertips on Tax Day when we each pay our donations to the state that makes life on the planet impossible yet infinitely distracting as the glittering radioactive orange floorshow host raves, his royal xenophobeness. Let's be OUT together, Trump, let's be gay and go away. I would gladly give you head on a desert island for the rest of my days if it would take you and all your cronies out of the kleptocratic oval office and you can even come in me as I change genders continuously and bear you infinite immigrant babies.

RED CONDOM IN THE RAMBLE

Daddy, where are we getting off?

    Time Square.

It's called Time Circle.

    No!

        If you're happy and you know it bite yourself.
        If you're happy and you know it bite your ear.

            My head sounds like a door.

    If you're happy and you know it
    and you really wanna show it,
    if you're happy and you know it
    bite your butt, your feet, your nuts.

But ten thousand years ago we were still basically kids. How often do you get to say that. Crabgrass and wind percussiveness like brushsticks. We met on the inner Met Museum steps which were a pickup place for cruisers like us but we met a philosopher guy there who just wanted to probe life's problems with us so we soon said goodbye and went among the grey Greek statues to acquire our evening's quota of zero gravity sex.

*Sexual fluids are exchangeable
I vow to exchange them all*

*Sexual fluids are transmittable
I vow to cure them all*

*Alien signals are relatable
I vow to relay them all.*

I went to Yugoslavia for coffee and came back four days later with a backpack full of ancestor entrails and no one even stopped me at CUSTOMS they just shot me full of machine gun bullets. Get up, Filip Marinovich, we will all have to jump out of whatever flight or story we find ourselves on when the towers burn again in New York Afghanistan

*O to never feel a living penis inside me
Only the encondomed cucumber up me
O to never feel myself unsheathed inside a living vagina
To be fucked only by disease
And the fear of transmission
HIV-positive Buddha HIV-negative Buddha
HIV-curing Buddha*

OM Maitreya awakener from the future
Aboard the Mars colony bound
Earth evacuation space station
Funny running into you at Whole Foods Organ Traffic Market
And feeling our embrace bloom twice inside of five minutes
We don't need to get tested we did it fully clothed
Rustling in our winter coats like takeout bags of whitest plastic

PIGEONTIMACY
an urban haibun

        the pigeons are reading
        the aeneid
        in the airshaft

yes the pigeons have come near us
like they never have before

a sidelong glance
at the fearful district of intimacy
to let it come into focus
sidewise perhaps kinder

but the pigeons are scaring me

I've never seen so many in the airshaft
call the bird interpreter
get me birdterpreter on line one

the bird interpreter is busy
at intimacy with worms limestone geysercufflinksfoam

just to get very portmanteau about it intimacy
invites speechtrains and wordslobstacles
of the ganesha variety of laughter

my friend conrad says ganesha is placed at the start of temples
the entrance
so you laugh as you come in

ganesha overcomes obstacles
you can have your head knocked off
by your father
because you love your mother and are sensitive
queer and feminine
pathetically intimate and intimately pathetic
snow flakes falling queerly and queerly falling
over the fast intimacy that feels so fake

if you slow down how does it change
if you unslouch how does the spinal antenna receive it

cecilia says theres so many pigeons now
I've never seen this many before

is it a sign I ask

of course it is a sign of
climate change and freezing temperature
pigeons cuddle in the airshaft

pigeontimacy dear
today two pigeons were mounting mating humping
on my air conditioner
and it was theirs at last
birds reclaim cooling unit
now naturally cool
chlorofluorocarbon free
refrigerator earth
new york city pigeon totem
and taboos of intimacy
abound in green purple darkblue feathers

*"we don't fly south in the winter
in order to torment you better
we the karmabirds
birdfruit of your actions
will wake you up with our warbling war
to remind you of the war you wage on each other every day
how full is it of obstacles
you don't know how to embrace
we embrace the obstacle of cold
by loving each other in the airshaft
but it's not utopia
we compete for each other
two males will fight
for the female mate
we pigeons don't have words for genders
to confuse us
we gather three at a time on a grey airconditioning perch
and two will fight while the third watches
one will be wounded and frightened off or killed
and two will remain to consummate
and make new pigeon tormentors of intimacy city new york
we the sentinel beings decree it"*

so the pigeon chorus speaks

one day I saw a dead pigeon
on the airconditioner directly opposite
the bedroom window of me and cecilia
its dark blue back to us in the snow

what is this an omen of
om

pigeontimacy
how do you embrace the dead battling mating calling singing pigeons
when you play the winter shut-in
in the ryokan hermit tradition
pretend
you pretentious pigeon with keypad
blurt out your own cooing tap tap tap tap tap
and bumble into the jam

wednesday night of this week
I invited my father to my poetry reading
and he came
and rather than do the usual thing of reading poems off paper
I flipped through my new book
and improvised live composition
rearranging chance lines as I encountered them
in the flipping pages

in this fun embarrassing intimate action
it helps to remember sensei's
"read it as if someone else wrote it"
and "it's none of my business what I write"
in the time of making it up live
it is indeed someone else doing it
someone I'm becoming who I don't know yet
who I'm curious about
what will she say next
me

guillaume apollinaire knew it
garconniere in french means bachelor pad
boyplace
but he intuited the sexism in that
and renamed his attic apartment
pigeonnier
because he was a pigeon and knew it
beyond gender
beyond the gender of a doubt
beyond the top to the other side wakened pigeon slide
and flight

coo coo coo

and after the reading
I went out with my father
and two friends
to dinner
to celebrate and talk and laugh
my father did what he often likes to do in these situations
embarrass me
he said
    "well you didn't have any stage presence tonight
    your flipping the pages was very distracting
    you didn't do it loud like ginsberg
    you were staring off into space
    you weren't your usual actor self"

my eyes welled up with rage as I
quietly told him in front of my two friends:
I'm working on coming from a quiet place

really what he was saying was
how could you be so soft feminine and pathetic
be a man
I'm a man you're a man
continue the man tradition

I'm not a man
not a pigeon
identity is very funny
perhaps I'm intimacy
and quiet is a way to see how I'm becoming
not a fixed point for an abusive father
to orient himself with a map he draws up and frames
and nails to curious furniture on golgotha landfill

the father said he understood but quickly forgot
what with that night's later
internet chaser of digitized newspapers
and televized sports recaps
in a high up apartment pigeons can't reach
it's so quiet in there
you can hear yourself think
so in terror you turn the tv up higher
and stuff your ears with purple earplugs father sleep

I was so angry with him wednesday night
and thursday friday
tonight I don't care

I gave my friend elizabeth a copy of my new book
she said it's so conservative and small
usually your books are messy and bigger

I asked her are you being my father now
or are you serious

        no I mean it

why am I getting this this week twice

        when people know you a long time
        they develop fixed ideas about you
        and they are wrong

when someone abuses you
and you absorb abuser
to stop pain and horror
you feel genitally
end daily negotiation
with abuser you became
to stop survivor pain
by talking to yourself
intimately

DEAR MOM

I cruise the Ramble
for poppenjay muscle
thunder the same roof
as birds why not
cruise them Bibliana

ice underfoot
                grab the fence
for dear epistolary practice

we've heard
Theory Bird
now let
Praxis Cardinal
speak of
twig and hay
nest built up
under the flightpath of
winter blitzkrieg Rilke pilot
dropping poems

I sign
  up
 to be a
     target
    Mom

I like men and men to kiss
when latex flowers bloom
and tourists take bird snapshots
I weep for Ramble lovers
who died in the Eighties
and lie under tundra crust

I want to kiss
the reddish-grey female
bright red male cardinal
airmail sent to you Mom
unsend send back

you say you don't understand

walk the Ramble
let it translate
beak to beak
we're moulting
under teabag trees

    drink from the
        teacup you hold out
since we're both
        teetotalers now

I want to drink
a palmfull of snow
with a shot of
dark rum poured into it
        just looking at snow
will have to do for now
until I'm snowblind
Oedipus killing unknown man
in roadside argument

Dear Mom
when you receive
this letter
picture me

in bed between
a girl and boy
your son
Lucky Pierre Reverdy
between Queen and King
I'm a Queen

        EXCUSE ME SIR SORRY TO BOTHER YOU
        I'M HERE FOR BOYS AND GIRLS OF
        AMERICA CAN YOU MAKE A DONATION

Queen of Hearts Spades Clubs Diamonds
Queen in a blue suit
Birthday Suit Queen
I swing
if you don't walk through
the swinging door now
when will you
the life promised us
after this one is
Nil
this is your son
Nilip Marinovich speaking

FOUR DAYS IN BELGRADE

JFK AIRPORT DINER WITH MOTHER

What's in that enormous suitcase of yours?

>My typewriter
>wrapped
>in sweatpants.

I don't know if your aunt
will let you pound that
at night.

>Mom,
>Belgrade was bombed
>44 times
>in the 20th century—
>>my typewriting
>>will not be heard
>>by the sleeping
>>but the dead
>>who don't mind
>>but help out
>>with a third hand on the keys
>>that shines.

MY AUNT ARCHITECTURE

3AM Belgrade I sob at your round diningroom table you ask me:

> "Would it help if I beat you up?
> Would it be Christmas then?"

coming back to Belgrade
my grandparents
continue to be dead
so how could I see them?

Grandfather speaks to me on the plane
from Zurich to Belgrade:
"Everybody will
remember to live in paradise today."

When I land
I can't see anyone waiting for me
where Grandfather used to stand in the first row to greet me
an airport sign:

> *IF YOU ARE NOT SURE OF WHETHER
> YOU HAVE SOMETHING TO DECLARE
> ENTER THE RED CHANNEL.*

I enter the green channel
the guards look at me
walking my enormous green
rollaway duffelbag
and do not stop me.

I text Uncle Unexpected
"Arrived.
I'll see you soon in the painful language"

    Puns are untranslatable —
  do you know Serbian —
dear reader —
do you consider yourself superior for not knowing it?

Who would want to know the language of a violent warmongering race?

Yes exactly who would want to know American English?

OVER INTERNATIONAL CELLPHONE

    Mom asks
    What are you scared of

        I hear voices of the dead in my head
        like free wireless

            you can't keep doing this

concrete
place
razed

    the floods destroyed Yugoslavia again after the bombs

    the flood did not not ask anyone

        are you Bosnian Croatian or Serbian

EMAIL FROM BELGRADE

Dear Julien,

I heard my grandfather on the flight from Zurich to Belgrade tell me everything's going to be okay.
It really did sound like his voice coming from the sky not my head and I realized these were the same flightpaths taken by so many warplanes over Belgrade
bombed in the 20th century more times than I can count one history book said "Belgrade rose from the ashes 39 times."

But my grandfather's voice was encouraging so I thought everything would be okay.
When I landed I felt lucky because nobody checked my bags and indeed I had nothing to declare so why would they but you never know here
you could disappear and not know about it till you read it on the news how you're dead
it could happen that fast like I said check your body at the airport
if you want to survive here unscathed
the invisible scalpel enters sideways and etches the signatures of oil magnates
on the inner walls of your skull.

The Ottoman Empire had a tradition of constructing walls of skulls
to chill the populace and make them obey
we have dollars for this same purpose
back "home" in the big glass domeland
of keggers shopping markets and a la carte bumper cars

"Show message history" no thank you

and when I landed and dragged my too heavy wheeled duffle bag
through customs and out to the greeting place
where I usually see my grandfather standing in the front row
waving to me in a big broadbrimmed straw sunhat
or my aunt smiling and waving with her long red hair
I saw no one

I wandered around in a quiet panic outside where I was propositioned by a huge grey cabbie
I went back in and finally spotted my uncle who I can barely recognize
who I call Unexpected in my poems to make it a mythos mouth I can speak through
not adhering to the facts of journalist ant vanity
and he has a big red rash behind his silver beard and looks like he might fall over dead
at any second
and he said "When did you come I didn't even see you just five minutes ago
okay let's go."
And we laughed at the sign in the parking lot

    PAY ON FOOT

and he told me how the country is in ruins and Eagle Hills of the United Arab Emirates wants to buy the land
on the Sava river and call it
The Belgrade Waterfront
and turn it into the Balkan version of
The Williamsburg Waterfront

and there was Merman Realtor on the side of the road
and the taxi driver village picnicing in the shade of cypresses by the airport
and all the NATO bombed buildings still standing on stick legs matchstick peglegs
and Uncle Unexpected said "The country is ruins
all these signs

   INVEST IN SERBIA

but no one has money to do absolutely anything."
First the war then the war then the war and now the floods. The flood didn't ask "Excuse me are you a Serbian a Bosnian or a Croatian person
so I can decide whether to tear the shingle roof off your house and stuff it in the bottom of
the Adriatic sea,"

and then he dropped me off at my Aunt Vesna's,
didn't come up, rather coldly said
"It's right there
the elevator
take a left and then when you get to the fifth floor
take a u-turn to your aunt's apartment."

And I went up in the elevator with my too heavy suitcases
elevator for two people at most pulled up by ropes creaking along the way
I could see the concrete floor dividers between the floors
and prayed I wouldn't get stuck the bags were so heavy

and my aunt welcomed me and immediately started setting
the table for a rich lunch of cheese pie my favorite I'd asked
for and then meat and soup
"Should I heat it up again yes this is what you asked for
now you must eat ha ha ha,"

The crocodile who breastfed me today got a son very easily

I'm a tiny little crocodile crying with flooded roof shingles
on my back
green with the emerald pastry flakes Grandma baked for
my spine to glisten and heal in
after the carrying of too heavy bags
why did I think I would need all those books
I didn't know my inner eyelids would be opening their frosty
encyclopedias
with the green children running out of the pages
to thump me on the throat and sing a song for boats to
cross the river
and every one finishes first in the regatta race
a miraculous first time fiveway tie in the Balkan states
and peace at the last

and then my Aunt Nena came in to visit and said
"My how strange you look to me in that beard I never saw
you like that before."

"Why of course you have Auntie I've been wearing it this
way for years."

I asked her how she was
and she said
"Well how I am
Not very well but it is okay
hahahahhaha,"
She laughed exactly like my grandmother who died and who to my surprise
is not here and neither is my grandfather

I accept that they died but why aren't they here to welcome me nevertheless
and where is that apartment they lived in where I stayed every time I came here
and which my idiot povertyridden Uncle Unexpected and Father Fearless
sold and dismantled and took the old boiler out of.

Where am I. What city is this.
What country, Friends, is this.
Is there a friend here. Oh, my Friends, there is no friend.
A Greek quotation
chiseled into a brick so the salamander can glide across it.

The pathetic nature of feeling
most excited about writing here
but not being able to live here
the continuous present it is
gives me short breathing lessons
until I am hyperventilation itself
playing tennis in Washington tomorrow and then home court in Toronto
there's no place like home

home is where the breath is
home is my diaphragm
put a diaphram in my ear
and fuck me there so I won't have kids

and I gave my apologies to my aunts and said
"I don't know what my name is,"
and went to bed
and my Aunt Nena said "Oh well thank God,"
meaning of course you don't know what your name is
you haven't slept in 24 hours.

So I tried to sleep from two in the afternoon to midnight but couldn't do it
got up many times to pee
from drinking three liters of tapwater filtered to avoid dehydration
and I went to the kitchen
told my aunt everything
how I called my mother crying and commanded her to book me
on the first
return
flight
leaving Belgrade
for Zurich and New
York
and now I'm looking at myself with some disdain
I don't know if I'll ever recover from
oh yes I just did with a breath

fuck disdain what did it ever do but give people ulcers
and I told my aunt how the flight is booked I'm leaving in
two days

now it's the end of the second day I only have tomorrow
to see people
my family
who I miss so much
and who I came here to reconnect with but found myself
overwhelmed completely
by the presence of the dead choking me and blessing
me in the same present
space

outer outer outer

and inscaped gardening I'm crying at the kitchen table
to my Aunt Vesna "This is the first time I've been here since
my grandparents died and it's so hard."
"That I can understand," she says
and I felt better just hearing that

and she said "A person should love himself
but not in a jinx way
but really love and respect himself by trying to help others.
To find yourself in the right job is the greatest art
and to know who you are and to not live toward
expectations of others
but to naturally be who you are and everything flows
easily from that."

And I wondered if my cousin her daughter had told her I'm gay
because I had confessed to that cousin that I'm bisexual
and I wondered if I wasn't being chastized by my aunt
but what happens when you try to love and respect yourself
but you are so many selves you don't know
how to satisfy them all because they will not accept anything
but total union of extremest opposites polarities tripolarities
and I went to bed and took a Nyquil which mercifully put me to sleep
after a half hour of hearing voices of Americans babbling
and me trying to spell Czechoslovakia backwards.

TRIPTYCH
IN CAPRICORN, AQUARIUS, AND PISCES

ABSENT SOPHIA

I know what open physical Grace was trying to do: the yoyo ahead of things spins so fast that in starting this relationship, whatever, we talk about it. You can tell Elizabeth. Everything I tell you is done to impede death. And Sophia knows that: whatever Elizabeth says is with an agenda. Open privacy. Always on defense. Piracy. Pirana. Pinata. Oedipus with his red pink yellow blue feelings outside preaches: "Parade Float Judgement Creature, ready for Micturition Ammunition, listening hard by, do you copy, over." No response. You need to have an ongoing relationship with yourself, Hamlet. You have a different right course in every single port and a motherfatheruncle ranunculous nuncle who tries to control laughter. You know how you need to be reminded of things. Everytime I clear out of the field, therapy doesn't continue, I'm done. I liked going this time around.

Sophia's not home for the weekend, where is she? Your own child. Triangulate. The icebergs that float out of the polar womb of triangulation. Skinbag visit. Is that like skinbag visiting privilege? When I entered I had to deal with Manson the dorm master at Thorne Dormitory. When I entered I had to deal with Manson the dorm master at Thorne Dormitory. But don't take advantage of me by calling me at 5:30 in the morning to pick up your junk. I have a party tonight: it's a family party. No parties no nothing. Work out the transportation since you're a shot put now. You would hope you would be an adult about it. Don't get annihilated with inhalation without exhalation. I'm starved for sexhalation. The adult part is you're on. This is me wanting to be with you. And at the same night there's a party. Sunday hangover triage. Me dealing with a hangover version of Sophia. Hangoversion bangoversion lalangoversion.

Perplexity will follow you wherever you go and whenever you stay home. If I'm lunch, he's only eighteen. Do you want to come over this weekend? It's Parent's Weekend and the Headmaster almost expels me for publishing critiques of the school administration during Desert Storm. Elizabeth said with her mouth "What is she doing here," as if I'm a piece of trash. We're so fortunate on a cellular level. Seeing my take on it, Homeworld Cyanide Cicada Half-the-Battle Ram came in his pants, north of the compassalamander taildial falling off with the poured out salt from the pear tree. Pink blue yellow green severance pencilcase.

This has been the worst year of my life the worst. I know and I don't want to demean that. Elizabeth's got a lot of demons and that's it, there's no more coparenting. It's really nice not dealing with Wisdom on a daily basis. Nice and tight, nice and light, must be the relationship with Sophia, because if she feels like she can't call home base, she's going to dissolve and absorb the bottom of the tequila bottle like a worm. It doesn't seem that way, it needs to be said outloud, I'm being honest from the outside. You need to be honest with your homely selfie and undress in front of it and give your knees to it: kneel and pray for your ability to parent.

My dorm master Manson came into my room and yelled "What's the matter you can't come say goodnight to me before bed anymore?" No: for my purpose here is to make war on all structures of the patriarchy, including westernized commodified time. My primary weapon is leisure. Hear it roar through the lesions sore: the lion in the pink chest birthmark will drag you back to Yugoslavia since you wish it, so you better get comfortable in its jaws. I got air conditioning installed in the lion's head. I ran out of honey, so for it I sent. Give me a handjob, Hamlet. You need to have an ongoing relationshipwreck on the shore of your igneous owl island with the lavatears running out of its eyeballs. The castaway you save may be your dorm master Manson. No one's looking out for you except your family album. Your parents forgot how to use memory so memory forgot them: the wake of assimilation from Balkans

into New England. It's not a given it's not a given. Vivienne Elizabeth Sophia assigned me homework: whatever you're preaching is Inferno. Listen your way back to Paradiso. What do you mean "back", you've never been there, that's why you don't believe in it. This is not a place in any trap. Bring something to this household: whenever you don't carry your weight it impacts this household. The problemsolver negotiator exacerbates the situation. You give your father another reason to escape reason. The wall of tranquiliy. The same bridge. All the conversations, like, this tender, have to feel unfiltered, but after your actions you have to actually feel that Valhalla axe in your head:

it can pass through the helmet, Hamlet. Hamlet Crab: come out of your shell and ring the bell for the waking up of the midnight Wassail Northeast March Club. When we go upstate we'll be a turn away from one drink. Three years sober: the worst time to drink a glass of tumbler away from the mother's presidents eleven years later. This is part of the reason you're in Missouri. There's a difference between chewing amber and teaching alphabet studies to a desk fresh from the wood shop. As long as you have a parent you can work around it, Hamlet.

As Hamlet's therapist not I only have hesitation in order to make hallways cheaper, I...[inaudible]. So I don't see Hamlet Sophia putting up a fight with Manhattan Denmark Soho Gap Gallon Galleon Captain when you tell me her mother wants to move with her. You're such a trooper, you're such a trooper, no, let me say it cos nobody else wants to say it, so let me say it with ten years of anger: he's become nothing other than a jealous exhusband.

Many people on eclipse days become owls and no one owns the owl not even the cigarette burn in the eleven of diamonds with the orange leaf beneath it just in time for fall nil autumn summer spring winter quartziferous timepiece clockface lice cloacal penguin opening to the north where ones escape into twoland for space and exercise of the psoas muscles, the twin souls trapped in the thighs until you free them with dancing. A history of dances. Structures of time. Now you're just rehearsing. But I'm ready for prehearsal time. But there's a lot of people vegetabling out of here. Just keep me away from the hearse, the wooden figure of Shepherd Holding Staff, naked as the day he was miscarried and grew up a magic jack o' lantern to light up the stoops of Greenwich Village where the bohemians now gather with Merman Realtor to find out how to take back their red brick heritage centers once lost to plutocrat entrails, red tape, and canapes.

You need to have an ongoing relationship with yourself, Hamlet.

Admiral Ophelia and I don't have time for that now, you have to delegate, prioritize, and spy freely enough to not be noticed by Deathcuffs. This being so—

So, we're trying to have a second kid, that's what I was telling you about. We're having trouble. The physical part is
I
Just found out
A
Possibility

Find out on a lover level

You're getting older quite fast.

It could be another bit of good news for the family
Or it could be

           patient daily decapitation of
Previousselves, sanely.

COUNT MOUTH

When I drink this juice it swings me around the room. They have a heat map and they act it out, the juice particles, with me in them. I am the ingredient Fingerlemon Lingam Conclusion. Occlusion is my game. I am is. I am a low cold front coming in through your shorts and low slung belt and the striped green suspenders you wear when you want to whip yourself. To punish yourself. It is too easy to be unkind. Later you just reward yourself with junkfood and tv night. Discipline means love comes in and you let it and it arranges the furniture and you listen to where the sofas land as they go thudding on the floor, or skid when towed by a speeding wild betusked extinct boar come back to show you what snorkeling is for with the snout of it the snout of what the snout of what the snout of it, what with the million smell openings you can sit over here.

There's plenty of us working here and we can all sit at the same table, silently besotted with each other. You have an intense ear to mind conductivity. Yes because I build a laptop in my skull, why should it be for the lap only? This would be anatomically incorrect and lapocentric. I think I have baby dementia, I'm starting to forget like my undead Uncle Dad in Denmarkish Connecticut. Ah, he's not with us in the picture. He's our fossil and one hundred ninety ninth person because Spontaneous Fossilization is invited to the event and it will show in the costume of an advent calendar long after Christmas, the east coast thing of not getting enough Vitamin D so Darth Vader steals into your room when you sleep and injects you full of some, he's a good guy really, like octodosing. I almost just passed out from the headrush juice. I will stop drinking it now. It is orange so I think it's healthy but when you are sleepless everything is concussion lovely. Concussion is so very lovely, who can say no to it later? The dental hygenist addresses me. Thank you, friendly torturer under whose instruments I disappear, come back, and almost pass out every visit. I wish I disappeared but that is not the case, you never give me gas, and I don't ask. Give me the gas! Will you read this and know? I want to laugh! Moon Hour. In my feed and inbox and inunreallife inundationstrife

I keep seeing DEATH like it's all anybody wants to talk about anymore. Who drinks it. Is it a smoothie that makes you pass out. My teacherfriend wrote to me and the whole class today and said: FOR YOUR WORKSHOP ON DYING. I am not in or leading a workshop on dying. I do not want to read or think about sticking a living will in the freezer for just in case or write a just in case I die this year here is my death poem, pre-ordered. No. I do not want to die this year or ever. In fact I will not. Ever. Die. A sure sign it's coming. Well, it will come anyway, for every body, but why must we always harp on it these days, and we are not harpers. Our voices croak we croak the croaker croaks the frog smokes on the stove. The apartment is going up in names: did you get that one? That one is funny. I need to prove myself. People don't want to know about their grades or graves and I don't want to know the bacteria count in my mouth, I want to kiss other people with even higher bacteria counts so we can all get immunized together by making out.

Not by keeping regular dental death tile visits. I don't go I'm going to Sweden or Denmark. I want to go to Denmark. Oh I heard a news from Denmark or somewhere, double latte to stay. It's a very friendly environment, Denmark, but it got that way from centuries of SOMETHING IS ROTTEN IN THIS STATE OF DENMARK. I doubt New York will last that long. One white coffee cup with a red cardboard heatshield band textured holder halo around its waist, I dip you and kiss you, we are dancing, coffee cup, and you do not care about my bacteria count mouth when you reach Denmark without me yet we will always be together in the memory right here make suds with Paul Medication in the dishwashing sink of nations, actions, orange juice bottle, black glasses case, reading glasses take me away, your thick lenses are strong sleds, when I ride one to the hill bottom, the other waits for me at the top so there's no dragging one back up but then when both sleds are at bottom with me I drag them both back up one in each hand and we go down again my two selves go down again now sametime happy sled glass crack against the silver Chevrolet towncar fender and let me get on a painkiller bender so I can listen to all these people talk about death and not hate them. Do they seriously think obsessing about death means not squandering their life. No. People lack the courage to talk about love and what and who they secretly desire most and by people and they I mean I, ai ai io io, ai ai, sky yoyo moon waxing to full eclipse light in the bull soon gone lion high and raging on the stage above the buildings red and black and grey and the cement steers with limbs scissoring above on elliptical machines in the well lit student discount gym. So what are these secret desires you hide? I want to make love with everyone alive and die.

SCHOOL OF SILENCERS

The Dean made the announcement for your funeral today over email. No flowers. Here at AWP Tampa it matters. Oh excuse me I didn't know who I was sitting with. This will be awkward honey to take me to the opera with. Who was it who told me NONE OF YOU HAVE THE MORAL AUTHORITY TO WRITE POLITICAL POETRY. Who does? a student asked. Stanley Kunitz, you said. A decade later your poem was in an anthology of political poetry along with the poems of your peers and students. Moral authority is taken not given. But how you poisoned us to make us find that out. Or we found out our own way whether you wanted us to or not. Or some of us did not and lie buried. How you plugged your ears with your fingertips and yelled LA LA LA LA LA as I tried to tell the class about Gertrude Stein, how she was not just "existential angst" as you called her, but eros empowerment female verbing replacing the phallic noun hoard of war. You did not want to learn and you humiliated me when I tried to learn and teach publicly at the seminar table, the butcher's chopping block, and I refused to be your pig slop. I refuse still. And now every one is competing on Facebook to see who will mourn you more, O how can we outgrieve each other in this blue and grey hollowed out gourd of a planet it really matters at AWP Tampa it really matters even more. Palm trees knock on your door waltz in and join the orgy. Wait let me wipe the chlorine out of my eyes or is that poetry. The recently deceased never would have even come into your consciousness, O Friendscape, had I not experienced their opus so voluminously at the beach clambake of the nerves of Rex Tyrranasaurus. Rex! Kyrie eleison Christe eleison. Now the student body will huddle together in shock and no one will dare say a word about how you mentally abused us. I never told any one except my terrible Lacanian analyst Onan about how at the graduation party for our class I offered you a fresh spring purple tulip I plucked from one of the campus gardens as a peace offering and you took the flower from my hand in your kitchen and whacked me with it on the left shoulder and said "Wham! I take away your powers!" I was angry not at you but at myself for believing it for a moment. I have no power for you to take away. Power can only be taken but you can't take it from me with a flower I'm going to send you flowers. Not the ones that grow from the earth but this one this mauve roarer that grows between my phone and fingers. Sendflower sendflower sendflower send. Rest dear teacher. I miss you and remain yours in the idiocy of our cosmic occupation in this ancestral infirmary of syllabic negotiations and disintegrating lungs in cigarette fumes of the tobacco saunas of our rooms, goodbye, dear wizard, no power for any of us when we all rejoin the breath and are not separate from it as bodies as wind as flowers as gyms full of stunning young new gymnasts testing out their limbs in the absence of our limbic systems. Refreshments will be served following a short service for the unheard.

ACKNOWLEDGEMENTS

Thank you to Lynne DeSilva-Johnson [Elæ] for all their inspiration, hard work, and patience.

Thank you to the editors of the magazines PRELUDE, Stu Watson, THE RECLUSE 13, Stacy Szymaszek, Simone White, Nicole Wallace, Laura Henrikson, LIVE MAG, Jeffrey Cyphers Wright, and FEBRUARY, Paul Legault, where several poems from THE SUITCASE TREE were first published.

Thank you to Jeffrey Joe Nelson and Jed Shahar, whose GREETINGS reading series has been a fantastic performance laboratory for new works for twenty years now.

Thank you to the Roshi Enkyo O'Hara, Joshin Sensei, and the entire Village Zendo Sangha.

Thank you to my comrades at Shakespearian Motley College.

Thank you to Lee Ann Brown and Tony Torn for giving Shakespearian Motley College a home at TORN PAGE.

Thank you to Alicia Jo Rabins for initiating me into THE GRIND and to Ross White for keeping it running so many years.

Thank you to Christina Davis for challenging me to write more about Occupy Wall Street and giving me a platform to perform the work.

Thank you to Trace Peterson and Paolo Javier for freestyling with me at Odessa.

Thank you to Eileen Myles for teaching me "Pathetic Inventory."

Thank you to CAConrad for teaching me in the midsummer blaze of Madison Square Park.

Thank you to Stacy Szymaszek for the Daybook Workshop.

Thank you to Julien Poirier for longtime poetry comradery.

Thank you to Cecilia Wu for my life.

Thank you to my parents for everything.

ABOUT THE AUTHOR:

Filip Marinovich is the author of WOLFMAN LIBRARIAN, AND IF YOU DON'T GO CRAZY I'LL MEET YOU HERE TOMORROW, and ZERO READERSHIP (all from Ugly Duckling Presse). His new book THE SUITCASE TREE is fabulously now in your hands from The Operating System. He conducts the ongoing poetry jam session SHAKESPEARAN MOTLEY COLLEGE at Torn Page in Chelsea Manhattan.

THE FRENETIC ARCHITECTURE OF DELIVERY: A CONVERSATION WITH FILIP MARINOVICH

.   .   ..

VARIATION ON A THEME BY RAM DASS

One is much
Suchness
We are in drag as the multiple

.   .   .   .

Greetings comrade! Thank you for talking to us about your process today! Can you introduce yourself, in a way that you would choose?

I'm Wolfman Librarian, AKA Loup Garou, the lariat on cue.

Why are you a poet/writer/artist?

I'm not. But rather, somewhere between wolf and human... the suchness...um...the myriad doth spring forth. . .the gazelle dolphin. . .yet another of the extinct pink on light blue elf cues to come in and take away my garden. Bring it back! I know it's not mine but bring it back anyway. Thou! Thourt that the one HUM. Yaourti in the Greek tradition...drizzled with golden prophecy beamhoney and walnuts...when I ordered this in Hania, Kriti--the waiter made bull snort noise and hoof stomp dance to show me it was coming. Pity it was not he coming upon my face for Thrace. Such dish: grace.

When did you decide you were a poet/writer/artist (and/or: do you feel comfortable calling yourself a poet/writer/artist, what other titles or affiliations do you prefer/feel are more accurate)?

Decoded in the frenetic architecture of delivery, ongoing and transforming through the unknown not-knowings.

What's a "poet" (or "writer" or "artist") anyway?
What do you see as your cultural and social role (in the literary / artistic / creative community and beyond)?

Songster of subversivest incest inroads into the royal family to make unrest a palimpsest of possibilities PRESENT.

Talk about the process or instinct to move these poems (or your work in general) as independent entities into a body of work. How and why did this happen? Have you had this intention for a while? What encouraged and/or confounded this (or a book, in general) coming together? Was it a struggle?

Never independent, toujours interdependent... interpenetrative interpretations unspooling the kite string of moment-- momentous gaucheries in the combat field alignment of stars alighting on the face at any given time, especially now as Mars the red orange swims through Pisces and splits the fish cord and those fish gotta find their own chord changes now based on faith let loose in the jamways--watch out for the pits--teeth break on that--but if you're not all gums by now perhaps you're not crunching hard enough on the fears and digesting them into the most delicious beers ever fermented in the mouth of Meerkat Lear.

Did you envision this collection as a collection or understand your process as writing or making specifically around a theme while the poems themselves were being written / the work was being made? How or how not?

Envision my soak as one long epic poke and being poked back in episodes--a top and bottom interlude catalog shifting through the thorough grammatical and etymological changes magnified through epistolary bifocals of the Epistolariat Committee of Letters (Komintern, sic.) A bathtub homecoming for Agamemnon is assured in these lines, nay, is rather precipitated, and the razor snowflakes of Klytaimnestra will slice that daughter-slaying fatherflesh of his so far down the bathtub drain we'll need a week's worth of Braino to blue it back up in the gurgle gargoyles of Neptune.

        No, but seriously.

No, but there is no no seriously. No separation between prose and poetry--no explaining explanations because no symmetry--nothing born--nothing dies--and yet here I smile with flesh full of flies--a hotel for death to escape into on one of its long hangover weekends when it must mend to become to the manor born once again with the bats. Is Batman in this? Because if not I refuse to read on! But perusal is imminent. You can tell by the tents under his eyes--Perusal's--that Perusal Arousal chap hath been in the Stacks studying so long the eyeballs goopdrip into the canvas and spandex banners anonymous arise--as long as the arising is listened to presently--the episodes unfurl and one is not separate from the other--such be the antidote of Poetry to the separation society of any organized Church and State Knot Constellation. Reclaim desire together as the myriad empowerments venturing forth into the embellishment mattress of nations--soon to be torn apart by us poet wolves for making love on the bare floor as the nerves hum under the tremendulous tablecloth of Frank O'Hara Candor Afterlife presently now reappearing as thoughtgong struck in the golden center by a music mallet with no hand attached to it.

Theme is discovered by accident on the way but also might be pre-ordained only to be thrown away in the winds of composition practice as the anthro chance chorus chimes in with its wise madness from every chiming coffee cup--we poets begin our lives in radness--thereof come dependency and recovery and Sadge adzes to cut through addiction rope and be whole again and listen patiently to the screams and whispers and songs of the holes even when they do you troll. And oh how they troll. But one must hear out and calm one's inner troll so's not to become it. So the Clairaudience of bliss presents itself to anyone willing to breath the breath with the breath. Unto breathlessness even. One emptiness. Empty of permanent abidance or New York State Residence. Fugue State Residents to come, welcome! Please step this way for our in the hills dance!

What formal structures or other constrictive practices (if any) do you use in the creation of your work? Have certain teachers or instructive environments, or readings/writings/work of other creative people informed the way you work/write?

Boa constrictors best avoided. Though the lines might become them. Most encouraging environment the one I created myself with a rag tag slowly discovered tribe: Shakespearian Motley College (which evolved from Reading Poets by Sun Sign and Queering Poets by Sun Sign)--these are "seminars" I teach, but really more like poetry jam sessions I conduct where we read poems together, aloud, by authors of whatever sign the sun happens to be in, (for example: Dickinson, Celan, and Myles for Sagittarius) and then we do "freewrites" and challenge ourselves to go as far into outer space as we can. Courage, candor, candelabra. To transgress against all our fears, emboldened by each other, playing in the band, writing to be banned and savored, wordspells as desire liberators.

Speaking of monikers, what does your title represent? How was it generated? Talk about the way you titled the book, and how your process of naming (individual pieces, sections, etc) influences you and/or colors your work specifically.

I saw a rollaway suitcase hanging from a tree growing out of the graves in front of St Marks Church and -- WHOOOSH -- Arrival of a Something. Investigate. Titles come after. All of this retrospectacle a fiction--what else could it be? I am not that person anymore. But the one now becoming is happy to be with you here and hopes you are having a good day--even in these our collapsing states of consciousness continually regenerated by faith and hopefully excercise regimen against whatever regime's in pretend power--to fete it out of the way--to let our feet ferry us where we play--far beyond all pepper spray! Occupay! Soleil coup coupe.

What does this particular work represent to you as indicative of your method/creative practice? your history? your mission/intentions/hopes/plans?

I'm curious what it might suggest to you and don't wish to stand in your way. That's true hospitality. Giving space. And time. And a stoop of wine. Or a stoop of any kind. Where are we going to congregate if not there? Only where it's monetary? We need spaces to play together without money vaccuuming everyone clean of eyes. No more eyesocket surprise. The one eyeball winks in the night flight to San Francisco tray table--but is it unfolded or folded back up--and who can tell when we've reached cruising altitude if there's endangered cruising shore. Let the extinct cruisers return and teach us how to score is not to score but to give and listen and dance between the orange cones until they are no more. "No obstructions in the mind because no-mind."--The Heart Sutra.

What does this book DO (as much as what it says or contains)?

This book loves you up if you ask it to.
It's yours to do with what you want to do.

If you sing it it might melt cage bars with you.
This book's no book
But a friend who talks by listening to you.
Crooner echo zoomlense in blue.

What would be the best possible outcome for this book? What might it do in the world, and how will its presence as an object facilitate your creative role in your community and beyond? What are your hopes for this book, and for your practice?

More Life.

Let's talk a little bit about the role of poetics and creative community in social activism. I'd be curious to hear some thoughts on the challenges we face in speaking and publishing across lines of race, age, privilege, social/cultural background, and sexuality within the community, vs. the dangers of remaining and producing in isolated "silos."

Poetry: made of, by, and for Interbeing--across all the arcs--throughout the allness in all its uniquenesses--celebrated openly--celebrated into existence again and again--by defiance and soulfullness and trust--today--yes. Now blesses us with its one chance and one and one again segments. Through all the messiness--the breath--thanks.

.   ..   .

WHY PRINT / DOCUMENT?

The Operating System uses the language "print document" to differentiate from the book-object as part of our mission to distinguish the act of documentation-in-book-FORM from the act of publishing as a backwards-facing replication of the book's agentive *role* as it may have appeared the last several centuries of its history. Ultimately, I approach the book as TECHNOLOGY: one of a variety of printed documents (in this case, bound) that humans have invented and in turn used to archive and disseminate ideas, beliefs, stories, and other evidence of production.

Ownership and use of printing presses and access to (or restriction of) printed materials) has long been a site of struggle, related in many ways to revolutionary activity and the fight for civil rights and free speech all over the world. While (in many countries) the contemporary quotidian landscape has indeed drastically shifted in its access to platforms for sharing information and in the widespread ability to "publish" digitally, even with extremely limited resources, the importance of publication on physical media has not diminished. In fact, this may be the most critical time in recent history for activist groups, artists, and others to insist upon learning, establishing, and encouraging personal and community documentation practices. Hear me out.

With The OS's print endeavors I wanted to open up a conversation about this: the ultimately radical, transgressive act of creating PRINT /DOCUMENTATION in the digital age. It's a question of the archive, and of history: who gets to tell the story, and what evidence of our life, our behaviors, our experiences are we leaving behind? We can know little to nothing about the future into which we're leaving an unprecedentedly digital document trail — but we can be assured that publications, government agencies, museums, schools, and other institutional powers that be will continue to leave BOTH a digital and print version of their production for the official record. Will we?

As a (rogue) anthropologist and long time academic, I can easily pull up many accounts about how lives, behaviors, experiences — how THE STORY of a time or place — was pieced together using the deep study of correspondence, notebooks, and other physical documents which are no longer the norm in many lives and practices. As we move our creative behaviors towards digital note taking, and even audio and video, what can we predict about future technology that is in any way assuring that our stories will be accurately told – or told at all? How will we leave these things for the record? In these documents we say:
    WE WERE HERE, WE EXISTED, WE HAVE A DIFFERENT STORY

- Elæ [Lynne DeSilva-Johnson], Founder/Creative Director
THE OPERATING SYSTEM, Brooklyn NY 2018

2019

Ark Hive-Marthe Reed
I Made for You a New Machine and All it Does is Hope - Richard Lucyshyn
Illusory Borders-Heidi Reszies
A Year of Misreading the Wildcats - Orchid Tierney
The Suitcase Tree - Filip Marinovich
We Are Never The Victims - Timothy DuWhite
Of Color: Poets' Ways of Making | An Anthology of Essays on Transformative Poetics -
Amanda Galvan Huynh & Luisa A. Igloria, Editors

KIN(D)* Texts and Projects

A Bony Framework for the Tangible Universe-D. Allen
Opera on TV-James Brunton
Hall of Waters-Berry Grass
Transitional Object-Adrian Silbernagel

Glossarium: Unsilenced Texts and Translations

Śnienie / Dreaming - Marta Zelwan/Krystyna Sakowicz, (Poland, trans. Victoria Miluch)
Alparegho: Pareil-À-Rien / Alparegho, Like Nothing Else - Hélène Sanguinetti (France, trans. Ann Cefola)
High Tide Of The Eyes - Bijan Elahi (Farsi-English/dual-language) trans. Rebecca Ruth Gould and Kayvan Tahmasebian
In the Drying Shed of Souls: Poetry from Cuba's Generation Zero
Katherine Hedeen and Víctor Rodríguez Núñez, translators/editors
Street Gloss - Brent Armendinger with translations for Alejandro Méndez, Mercedes Roffé, Fabián Casas, Diana Bellessi, and Néstor Perlongher (Argentina)
Operation on a Malignant Body - Sergio Loo (Mexico, trans. Will Stockton)
Are There Copper Pipes in Heaven - Katrin Ottarsdóttir (Faroe Islands, trans. Matthew Landrum)

2018

An Absence So Great and Spontaneous It Is Evidence of Light - Anne Gorrick
The Book of Everyday Instruction - Chloë Bass
Executive Orders Vol. II - a collaboration with the Organism for Poetic Research
One More Revolution - Andrea Mazzariello
Chlorosis - Michael Flatt and Derrick Mund
Sussuros a Mi Padre - Erick Sáenz
Sharing Plastic - Blake Nemec
In Corpore Sano : Creative Practice and the Challenged Body [Anthology]
Abandoners - L. Ann Wheeler
Jazzercise is a Language - Gabriel Ojeda-Sague
Born Again - Ivy Johnson
Attendance - Rocío Carlos and Rachel McLeod Kaminer
Singing for Nothing - Wally Swist
The Ways of the Monster - Jay Besemer
Walking Away From Explosions in Slow Motion - Gregory Crosby
Field Guide to Autobiography - Melissa Eleftherion

Glossarium: Unsilenced Texts and Translations

The Book of Sounds - Mehdi Navid (Farsi dual language, trans. Tina Rahimi
Kawsay: The Flame of the Jungle - María Vázquez Valdez
(Mexico, trans. Margaret Randall)
Return Trip / Viaje Al Regreso - Israel Dominguez; (Cuba, trans. M.Randall)

for our full catalog please visit:
https://squareup.com/store/the-operating-system/

deeply discounted Book of the Month and Chapbook Series subscriptions
are a great way to support the OS's projects and publications!
sign up at: http://www.theoperatingsystem.org/subscribe-join/

DOC U MENT
/däkyəmənt/

First meant "instruction" or "evidence," whether written or not.

noun - a piece of written, printed, or electronic matter that provides information or evidence or that serves as an official record
verb - record (something) in written, photographic, or other form
synonyms - paper - deed - record - writing - act - instrument

[*Middle English, precept, from Old French, from Latin documentum, example, proof, from docre, to teach; see dek- in Indo-European roots.*]

Who is responsible for the manufacture of value?

Based on what supercilious ontology have we landed in a space where we vie against other creative people in vain pursuit of the fleeting credibilities of the scarcity economy, rather than freely collaborating and sharing openly with each other in ecstatic celebration of MAKING?

While we understand and acknowledge the economic pressures and fear-mongering that threatens to dominate and crush the creative impulse, we also believe that ***now more than ever we have the tools to relinquish agency via cooperative means,*** fueled by the fires of the Open Source Movement.

Looking out across the invisible vistas of that rhizomatic parallel country we can begin to see our community beyond constraints, in the place where intention meets resilient, proactive, collaborative organization.

Here is a document born of that belief, sown purely of imagination and will. When we document we assert. We print to make real, to reify our being there. When we do so with mindful intention to address our process, to open our work to others, to create beauty in words in space, to respect and acknowledge the strength of the page we now hold physical, a thing in our hand, we remind ourselves that, like Dorothy: *we had the power all along, my dears.*

THE PRINT! DOCUMENT SERIES
is a project of
the trouble with bartleby
in collaboration with
the operating system

www.ingramcontent.com/pod-product-compliance
Lightning Source LLC
Chambersburg PA
CBHW030110100526
44591CB00009B/354